LIFE IN
REGENCY ENGLAND

(Overleaf) *The Prince of Wales at the Brighton Pavilion*

Life in

REGENCY
ENGLAND

R. J. WHITE

English Life Series
Edited by PETER QUENNELL

LONDON: B. T. BATSFORD LTD
NEW YORK: G. P. PUTNAM'S SONS

Made and printed in Great Britain
by William Clowes and Sons, Limited, London and Beccles
for the publishers
B. T. BATSFORD LTD
4 Fitzhardinge Street, Portman Square, London, W.1
G. P. PUTNAM'S SONS
200 Madison Avenue, New York 16, N.Y.

Preface

This is a book about the thoughts, feelings, and behaviour of the men and women who lived in Regency England rather than yet another book about 'Regency' style in building and the fine arts (although that comes into it). 'Regency' is a term which has a legitimate application to English life for some few years after the official term of the Regency came to an end in 1820, and I have accepted the hang-over quite freely, drawing the line firmly with the accession of Queen Victoria, who was born in 1819.

The authors to whose works I am chiefly indebted are recorded in the reading-lists at the foot of each chapter, and my special thanks are due to my wife who ransacked them on my behalf at a time when ill-health prevented my reading much. Without her assistance I could not have fulfilled my engagement with my publisher. But I alone am responsible for the book's opinions, and its errors and limitations.

This is a period especially rich in literary sources, and anyone who writes its history must pay tribute to Jane Austen and George Borrow, William Hazlitt and S. T. Coleridge, William Cobbett and Samuel Bamford, among others. Some of them, like Borrow, wrote when the Regency was over, but it was the time of their youth, and they always remained its sons and daughters. It will be plain how great is my own debt also to such authorities of the present century as Humphry House, Sir John Summerson, Sir Harold Nicolson, and Lesley Blanch.

I would like to thank Mr Peter Kemmis Betty of Messrs Batsford for his expert and devoted handling of the problems of illustration.

Elmdon   R. J. W.
Spring 1963

Contents

PREFACE vii

ACKNOWLEDGMENT x

LIST OF ILLUSTRATIONS xi

I Regency England 1

II The Lower Classes 21

III The Middle and Upper Classes 43

IV London 62

V Politics 85

VI Manners and Morals 102

VII Scenes from Provincial Life 117

VIII The Puritan Revival 138

IX The Dawn of the Age of Seriousness . . 151

INDEX 169

Acknowledgment

The illustration on page 2 is reproduced by gracious permission of Her Majesty The Queen.

The author and publishers wish to thank the following for the illustrations appearing in this book: the Trustees of the British Museum for the illustrations appearing on pages 9, 18, 28, 52, 56, 80, 83, 87, 96, 116, 146, 154, and 157; the Mansell Collection for pages 31, 94, 101, 110, 128, and 135; the Marylebone Cricket Club for pages 112–13; the National Portrait Gallery for pages 86, 92, 146, and 153; the National Gallery of British Sports and Pastimes for page 3; the *Radio Times* Hulton Picture Library for page 111; the St Marylebone Public Library for page 100; the Trustees of the Victoria and Albert Museum (Crown copyright reserved) for the frontispiece and pages 23 and 81.

The Illustrations

The Prince of Wales at the Brighton Pavilion *From a drawing by Robert Cruikshank* . . . . *Frontispiece*
The Prince of Wales' carriage-horses *From a painting by George Stubbs* 2
The racehorse 'Vandyke' *From a painting by H. B. Chalon, 1809* 3
A pedlar *From Pyne's 'Microcosm', 1808* 3
The London–Brighton stage-coach *From an engraving by Charles Hunt after W. G. Shayer* 4–5
A country-house gardener *From R. Phillips, 'The Book of English Trades', 1818* 6
Elegance and prosperity *Drawn and engraved by Henry Moses, 1823* 7
Stisted Hall, near Braintree *From an engraving by J. C. Armytage after W. Bartlett, 1832* 8
Duelling *Drawn and engraved by Robert Cruikshank, 1825* . . . 9
Gambling on a cock-fight *Painted and engraved by Henry Alken* . 10
A stage-coach *From a woodcut by Thomas Bewick* 11
The yard of a coaching-inn *From an aquatint by Henry Alken* . 12–13
Rolle Canal, near Torrington *From an engraving by T. Dixon after T. Allom, 1832* 13
The construction of the Highgate Archway *From a contemporary engraving* 14
Gurney's steam carriage *From a lithograph by G. Scharf, 1827* . 15
The craze for hobby-horses *From a contemporary sketch* . . . 15
A stocking-weaver 16
A shoemaker 16
    Both from R. Phillips, 'The Book of English Trades', 1818
A streetcryer *From a woodcut by Thomas Bewick* 17
A village smithy *From an aquatint after Thomas Rowlandson, 1808* 17
The Westminster rat-pit *From an etching by Theodore Lane, 1825* 18
Prisoners being carted off to execution *From an aquatint after Thomas Rowlandson, 1808* 19
A carrier's wagon *From a woodcut by Thomas Bewick* . . . 20

xi

Foundry-workers   *From Pyne's 'Microcosm', 1808*   22
A farm-labourer *From a contemporary sketch*   23
A farm-labourer's cottage   *From a painting by George Morland* .   23
A yeoman's farmhouse   *From Dugdale's 'England and Wales'* .   24
Threshing with flails   25
A plough team   25
   Both from Pyne's 'Microcosm', 1808
Reaping   *From a contemporary woodcut*   26
The farmworker's diet   *From Pyne's 'Microcosm', 1808* . . .   26
A yeoman farmer   *From a woodcut by Thomas Bewick*   27
The prosperous farmer   *From an etching by James Gillray, 1809* .   28
Calico-printing   *From R. Phillips, 'The Book of English Trades',*
   1818   29
Thomas Howitt, colliery-manager   *From a sketch by Mary Howitt*   30
Robert Owen's model factory at New Lanark   *From a contemporary*
   aquatint   31
Bricklayers   *From R. Phillips, 'The Book of English Trades', 1818*   32
A laundry maid   *From a painting by George Morland*   33
Spinning with a hand-jenny   *From R. Phillips, 'The Book of English*
   Trades', 1818   33
Power-loom weaving   *From an engraving by J. Tingle after T.*
   Allom, 1835   34
A Leeds collier   *From George Walker, 'The Costume of Yorkshire',*
   1814   35
Manchester cotton factories   *From an engraving after Samuel Austin*   36
Factory children   37
Cottage Industry   38
   Both from George Walker, 'The Costume of Yorkshire', 1814
A mill   *From a woodcut by Thomas Bewick*   39
A colliery   *From Pyne's 'Microcosm', 1808*   39
Bolton, an 'industrial' market town   *From an engraving after*
   Harwood, 1829   40
A market cross   *From Pyne's 'Microcosm', 1808*   41
A merchant   *From R. Phillips, 'The Book of English Trades', 1818* .   44
St Katherine's Docks, London   *From an engraving by H. Jordan*
   after Thomas Shepherd, 1829   45
A middle-class family   *From a watercolour by W. Pickett, 1811* .   46
An academy   *From a woodcut by Thomas Bewick*   47
The Burlington Arcade   *From a contemporary engraving* . . .   48
A linen-draper's shop   *From R. Phillips, 'The Book of English*
   Trades', 1808   49
Dressed for the country   *From a contemporary sketch*   50

The country gentleman 51
Shooting 52
   Both from contemporary woodcuts
'The savage enforcer of the Game Laws'   *From an aquatint after*
   Thomas Rowlandson, 1817 52
'Humane man-trap'   *From an ironfounder's catalogue* 53
The national sport: hunting   *From a woodcut by Thomas Bewick*   54
Rebuilding à la mode   *From an aquatint after Thomas Rowlandson,*
   1817 56
Afternoon tea   *Drawn and engraved by Henry Moses, 1823* . . 57
The Devonshire minuet   *From a contemporary sketch* 58
A musical evening   *From a contemporary woodcut* 58
Officer and gentleman   *From an engraving of 1807* 59
A physician 59
A clergyman of the Establishment 60
   Both from contemporary sketches
A domestic entertainment   *From a silhouette by Augustin Edouart*.   61
The City skyline, from Blackfriars bridge   *From a contemporary*
   print 63
The Egyptian Hall, Piccadilly 65
The Coliseum, Regent's Park 66
   Both from engravings by A. McClatchy after Thomas Shepherd, 1828
A villa in the Regent's Park   *From an engraving by W. Wallis after*
   Thomas Shepherd, 1827 67
Park Village East, Regent's Park   *From an engraving by W. Radcliff*
   after Thomas Shepherd 68
The Quadrant, Regent Street   *From an engraving by Thomas Dale*
   after Thomas Shepherd, 1827 69
Cumberland Terrace, Regent's Park   *From an engraving by James*
   Tingle after Thomas Shepherd, 1827 71
Regent Street, from the Quadrant   *From an engraving by W.*
   Tombleson after Thomas Shepherd, 1828 72–3
'Five O'Clock in Hyde Park'   *From an aquatint by 'C. H.'* . . 74
The Bank of England   *From an engraving by W. Wallis after Thomas*
   Shepherd, 1828 75
Entrance to the Regent's Canal, Limehouse,   *From an engraving by*
   E. J. Havell after Thomas Shepherd, 1828 76
The West India Import Dock   *From an engraving by T. Barber after*
   Thomas Shepherd, 1829 77
Lighting an oil lamp   *From a sketch of 1805* 78
Gas-works, near the Regent's Canal   *From an engraving by*
   McClatchie after Thomas Shepherd, 1829 78

THE ILLUSTRATIONS

The Regency Theatre, Tottenham Court Road *From an engraving after Jacob Schnebbelie* 79

The gaming-room of a London club *From an engraving after W. Heath, 1823* 80

The Cyprians' Ball at the Argyle Rooms *Drawn and engraved by Robert Cruikshank, 1825* 80

The Vauxhall Gardens *From an engraving after A. C. Pugin, 1804* 81

Charleys *From a contemporary sketch* 82

A punch-up with the Charleys *From an engraving after W. Heath, 1823* 82

The Press Yard, Newgate *Drawn and engraved by Robert and George Cruikshank, 1820* 83

A public execution *From a contemporary print* 84

Robert Stewart, Viscount Castlereagh *From a drawing by George Dance, 1794* 86

The House of Lords *Drawn and engraved by Robert Cruikshank, 1825* 87

Henry Addington, Viscount Sidmouth *From a lithograph by R. J. Lane after S. Catterson Smith* 89

John Scott, Lord Eldon *From an engraving by H. Wallis after Sir Thomas Lawrence* 90

Jeremy Bentham *From a silhouette by J. Field* 92

'The Peterloo Massacre' *From a sketch by Fogg, 1819* . . . 93

Francis Place *From a drawing by D. Maclise* 94

William Cobbet relieving the industrious labourer *Drawn and engraved by W. Panarmo* 95

Sir Francis Burdett at the Middlesex Election *From an etching by James Gillray, 1804* 96

Jeremiah Brandreth *From an engraving of 1817* 98

Orator Hunt *From a contemporary sketch* 99

The Cato Street Conspiracy *Drawn and engraved by Robert Cruikshank, 1820* 100

William Cobbett, M.P. *From a drawing by D. Maclise* . . . 101

A dandy at his dressing-table 102

A lady of fashion 103

The waltz 104

All from contemporary sketches

Domestic life of the aristocracy *Drawn and engraved by Henry Moses, 1823* 105

The Regent and his uncle *From a silhouette by Charles Rosenberg* 106

The Royal Pavilion, Brighton *From an engraving after W. Westall, 1829* 107

Regency à la mode *From a contemporary sketch* 108

xiv

A sparring match at the Fives Court *From a painting by T. Blake* 109
A prize fight *Painted and engraved by Henry Alken* 110
A game of cricket *From an etching of 1821.* 111
England v. Sussex match at Darnall *From an aquatint by Robert Cruikshank, 1827.* 112–13
A box at the opera *Drawn and engraved by Henry Moses, 1823* . 114
Ladies driving in Hyde Park *From a fashion plate of 1794* . . 114
Le Beau Monde *Drawn and engraved by Henry Moses, 1823* . . 115
Harriette Wilson *From a contemporary print* 116
Cottage ornée at Milton Abbot 119
A neo-Gothic country house, near Dawlish 120
  Both from engravings after T. Allom, 1830
Young ladies at home *Drawn and engraved by Henry Moses, 1823* 121
Boys skating *From a woodcut by Thomas Bewick* 122
Adults in miniature *From a silhouette by Augustin Edouart* . . 122
An academy for young ladies 123
Girls skipping 124
  Both from woodcuts by Thomas Bewick
A young lady *From Ackermann's 'Repository of the Arts', c. 1820.* 124
Children's games *From a fashion plate of 1832.* 125
'An English domestic interior' *Drawn and engraved by Henry Moses, 1823.* 126
A card party *From an aquatint after Thomas Rowlandson, 1820* . 127
The Montpellier Pump Room, Cheltenham *From an engraving after H. Lamb* 128
Bathing machines in Bridlington Bay *From George Walker, 'The Costume of Yorkshire', 1814.* 129
The sands at Worthing *From a painting by John Nison, 1808* 130–1
The Steyne, Brighton *From a print of 1828* 132–3
Hall's Library at Margate *From a print of 1789* 134
The morning promenade at Cheltenham *Drawn and engraved by Robert Cruikshank, 1823.* 135
The arrival of the Margate hoy *From an engraving by J. Hill after P. J. Loutherbourg, 1808* 136
A paddle-steamer *From a woodcut by Thomas Bewick* 137
A Wesleyan Chapel, Liverpool *From an engraving after G. and C. Payne* 139
A service in St Andrew's, Plymouth *From an engraving by T. Dixon after T. Allom, 1832.* 140
Dr Simeon, the evangelical preacher *From a silhouette by Augustin Edouart* 141
An improving book *From a woodcut by Thomas Bewick* . . . 142

The National Scotch Church, London   *From an engraving by W. Watkins after Thomas Shepherd, 1829* 144

Robert Owen   *From a contemporary sketch* 145

Title page of an early tract   *From ' The Shepherd of Salisbury Plain'* 146

William Wilberforce   *From a painting by Sir Thomas Lawrence* . 146

William Cobbett   *From a silhouette after a contemporary sketch* . . 147

A Sunday school   *From a woodcut for an educational tract* . . . 149

Sir Walter Scott   *From a silhouette by Augustin Edouart* . . . 152

Jane Austen   *From a contemporary silhouette* 153

'Tales of horror'   *Drawn and engraved by James Gillray, 1802* . 154

A London bookshop   *From an engraving after W. Heath, 1823* . 155

A lecture in the Royal Institution   *Drawn and engraved by James Gillray, 1802* 157

Humphry Davy, with his miner's lamp   *From a painting after Sir Thomas Lawrence* 159

Leigh Hunt   *From a drawing by D. Maclise* 160

Charity School, Gravel Lane, London   *From an engraving after Jacob Schnebbelie, 1822* 161

Primary education for girls   *From a woodcut by Thomas Bewick* . 162

The School Room at Eton   *From an engraving by J. C. Stadler after A. C. Pugin* 163

London University   *From an engraving by W. Wallis after Thomas Shepherd, 1828* 164

The Regent   *From a contemporary engraving* 167

I

Regency England

Strictly speaking, Regency England lasted from 1811, when King George III lapsed into incurable madness, until 1820 when the old king died and the Regent became King George IV. The term 'Regency', however, has become one of much wider application, and particularly as the name for a style in building, dress and the fine arts in general. It is known for its rather portentous Classicism and its playful Gothicism, its Grecian pillars, its flat façades, its toy turrets and pinnacles, its fissiparous stucco and its perforated ironwork. These features of the Regency scene belong to a period which extends both before and after the official dates of the Regent's government. Perhaps because his taste for and patronage of the fine arts is his best claim to be remembered, we continue to use his official title as the name for a style which he certainly did not inaugurate although it reached peak-production while he was titular head of the state. Nor is the name properly confined to a style of building or decoration. Regency England possessed a certain social flavour of its own, an individual quality of living, an atmosphere that can only be recovered with difficulty. It had a character, even a personality, which lingers on wherever its material records survive. It is perhaps the last truly historical age, in the sense that it is divided from us by a real chasm in time. The chasm came with the railways.

How are we to recapture the spirit of that age, to savour its quality, to breathe its air, to recover the nature of its experience, the very stuff of experience as its men and women knew it? It

1

is, strictly, impossible. It is possible to state a great many facts about its manners and morals; to quote its figures of mortality, its vital statistics. We can recount what it ate, what it wore, what it read, how it treated its women and children and animals. . . . But its life-quality eludes us, save as it comes to us like a flavour, a perfume, a clamour of voices, from a heath, a kitchen door, a busy street, in an unapprehended moment of revelation, while we look at some memorial in print or paint or stucco-pasted brick. Look at a picture of a racehorse by Seymour or Stubbs or Morland. Look at Stubbs' famous portrait of the Prince's carriage-horses and equestrian servants. For this was the age of the horse, par excellence; 'the noblest friend of man', richly caparisoned, docked of tail, with burnished coat in fine condition by reason of a diet far more nourishing than that of millions of two-legged beasts of burden. Everyone who went anywhere at speed went on, or behind a horse. Twenty-five thousand rural blacksmiths waited on this equine aristocracy in shoes alone. Considerably more waited upon its feeding and watering, its housing and its health and its daily exercise.

There, in the middle of the Regency scene, stands *Vandyke*, or *Atlas*, or *Careless*, his barrel like a gutted herring, his tiny pointed

The Prince of Wales' carriage-horses

The racehorse 'Vandyke'

head protruding from his raking shoulders, his stilt-like legs stalking under his sinewy quarters; a cross between a snake and a stag. Overhead arch the vast empty skies of East Anglia. Beyond stretch the endless solitudes of the heath. *Vandyke*'s owner might be adorned in cutaway coat and top-hat, but his daily companion is a stable-lad-in fustian, his slave who feeds him, waters him, exercises him. Such a horse never went to Newmarket in a box on road and rail. His stable-companion and slave never went to school. He probably wandered on to Newmarket Heath, like Tom Holcroft, after tramping the country with his parents, peddling pins and needles, tapes and garters, or begging a living from door to door. Soon he will be on the roads again, this time as a strolling-player. He will scribble pieces for the theatre at Covent Garden, notably *The Road to Ruin*. After his death, William Hazlitt will write his life. No one will write the life of *Vandyke*, but his portrait will hang in a hundred inns up and down England, which is nearly as fine a form of immortality, as Hazlitt would be the first to agree. This is life as it was lived then, by multitudes of men and beasts: itinerant, full of chances and changes, scarcely noticed by government—unless by a parish beadle, a preventive man or a press-gang. . . . No one counted them until 1801, and even then reluctantly, for did not Holy Scripture warn against the numbering of the people? The census found there were round about thirteen million of them in the first year of

A pedlar

the nineteenth century: at least twice as many of them as had been computed half a century earlier. As for weighing them, Thomas Hardy, who was born as late as 1840 and didn't die until 1928, would never submit to be weighed in his life because it was unlucky.

There was something radically untamed about Regency England. It was a quality that D. H. Lawrence believed to have survived in the countryside of his father's midland England. It was celebrated in the England of Queen Victoria by George Borrow when he wrote of his youth under the Regent and George IV. It was the spirit of the England of the tents, the horse-fair, the prize-ring, the tramping pedlars and mumpers, the Flaming Tinman and Isopel Berners. England was still a land of wide commons and lost hamlets, sleepy country towns and sudden violence. The man-made things in such a landscape were often as beautiful as the things made by nature. Their beauty was something inherent in the care and craft that had gone to the making rather than something consciously added

The London–Brighton stage-coach

or the studied beauty of a style. And this was true, very often, of the latest and proudest products of men's hands. 'Next after a fox-hunt, the finest sight in England is a stage-coach just ready to start', wrote William Cobbett in 1818. He would admit that a great sheep or cattle fair was a beautiful sight, 'but in a stage-coach you see more of what man is capable of performing. The vehicle itself, the harness, all so complete and so neatly arranged; so strong and clean and good. The beautiful horses impatient to be off. The inside full, and the outside covered in every part, with men, women, children, boxes, bags, bundles. The coachman, taking the reins in one hand and his whip in the other, gives a signal with his foot, and away they go, at the rate of seven miles an hour, the population and the property of a hamlet.'

The stage-coach was not an antique achievement, but the latest thing in man's conquest of space and time. Few could resist its verve and its visual splendour. 'It is a very animated and enlivening spectacle', wrote Mr Gray in his *Microcosm*

leaving the 'Bull and Mouth', Piccadilly

(1803), 'it raises very pleasing ideas in the mind of the observer who has studied the progress of society. There is something in this coach so impressive and attractive, that as it drives along the road, or through a town, it draws every eye towards it, and the sound of it immediately fills the windows. In many villages the children still take off their hats and shout when it passes.'

And when Charles Dickens began to write for the public in the early railway age of the 1830s, it was of the coaching days, so lately passed away, that he first wrote, carrying on (as Chesterton put it) 'a rank, rowdy, jolly tradition of men falling off coaches before the sons of Science and the Great Exhibition began to travel primly on rails—or grooves'. In later life, when he wanted to entertain visitors at Gad's Hill with something special, he would turn out 'a couple of postilions in the old red jacket of the old red royal Dover road', and drive his guests round Kent in the fashion of older and better days.

England was never to be so beautiful again. The canvas was still largely unspoilt, and the men were at hand to work upon it. Never has England been so rich in fine and handy makers. From the tying of a cravat to the designing of a palace or a country house there was a hierarchy of artificers, from Beau Brummel to John Nash and Sir John Soane, Wyatt, Smirke, Wilkins and Papworth. To blend the landscape with the buildings there was Humphrey Repton, and Endsleigh, and Loudon, and a whole profession of gardeners. When the buildings were up and the gardens laid out, there were legions of decorators to adorn the interiors with pilasters and peristyles, fine hangings in crystal and velvet, elegant furniture in the great native traditions of Sheraton and Vile. . . . The people who moved among these artefacts could look to futurity at the hands of

A country-house gardener

6

Lawrence and Raeburn and Chantrey. More modestly they could call upon Mr Meirs in the Strand and perpetuate their profiles in the homely silhouette. To a later age they look like Little Englanders, engrossed snugly in their charming landscape, scarcely lifting their eyes from the confines of the hall, the terrace, the assembly rooms of the county town, the counting-house, the covert, the London square, the college, the rectory and the home-farm. In fact, however, they were

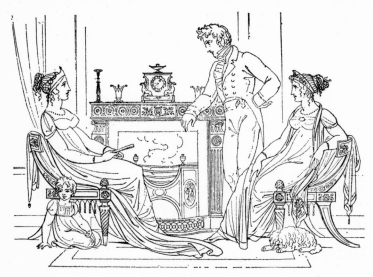

Elegance and prosperity

making Old England into the Great Britain of the Victorians. Patrick Colquhoun's *Resources of the British Empire* was published in 1815.

In aggregate, the English were immensely rich, and most of the national wealth lay in private hands, hence the ready resources available for beautification. Beauty has to be paid for, especially the kind of beauty in stone and metal, timber and glass, which flourished in the Regency. When foreigners visited the country, as they did a great deal after the war, and wrote down their observations, it was England's commercial

A Regency country house: Stisted Hall, near Braintree, Essex

wealth that most impressed them; and not only the actual wealth, but the concern for wealth, the inveterately commercial habits of the people, high and low, and their commercial standards of value. Prince Pückler-Muskau, coming here in the autumn of 1826, thought Nash's architecture 'monstrous', and was far more impressed by the landscape-gardening. It was, however, the Englishman's inflexible routine in his business life, and the universally valid 'habits of Business', that impressed him most of all. The amount of work done, and the universal deference to wealth, struck the Prince as the chief characteristics of the English. The Continental visitor could see all the splendid building he wanted in Paris or Rome. He came to England to see the gardens, the richly cultivated farms, and most of all to see how the English managed to be so rich and comfortable. To the visitor, Regency England was what the United Provinces had been in the seventeenth century, and what the United States have been in the nineteenth and twentieth, the affluent society, the successful people with the recipe for wealth, comfort and freedom.

And like all rich and successful people, the English of the Regency had a fairly fat streak of vulgarity. They were crudely vigorous, and they had *brio*: a quality which generally looks like vulgarity to the unsuccessful and the tired. Their gusto extended to their manners. They let themselves go. They laughed and wept with an abandon which was soon to be

8

regarded as reprehensible or Continental. Nelson's immortal scene in the cockpit of the *Victory* was no isolated instance of a dying fall. Something habitual and unrehearsed was dying with Nelson: the dramatic, or melodramatic, gesture of a race which habitually wore its heart on its sleeve—and at the same time kept its powder dry. The sailors who brought Nelson home in pickle did not fail to drink the spirits when the *Victory* ran dry ('broaching the Admiral' they called it), because, they said, their hero would have so wished it. What would our ancestors have said about Members of Parliament who shed tears in the House of Commons, William Wordsworth once asked. The answer is, they would have done the same, like Cromwell and Sir Thomas More. Wordsworth, as Coleridge said, was 'all man'. Moreover, he lived to see the dawn of the Age of the Stiff Upper Lip and the reformed Public Schools. Anyway, Regency Englishmen went their own way. They not only shed tears in public. They fought duels in private, or beyond the eye of authority, for they were *hors du loi*. Pitt fought Tierney on Wimbledon Common in 1798. Castlereagh met Canning on Putney Heath in 1809. Wellington fought Winchilsea at Battersea in 1829. And there were later cases. But the farcical duel of Nathaniel Winkle and Dr Slammer in *Pickwick* may be said to show what was happening to the solemnities of that aristocratic ritual by 1837, the first year of Queen Victoria.

Duelling

Perhaps, after all, these things were not solemnities, but rather the uttermost lengths to which a notoriously gambling nation chose to carry their passion for gaming. The English would lay odds on anything from a horse-race to the gambols of a couple of flies on a window-pane.

The fast mail-coaches which started to dash up and down to London after 1784, when John Palmer secured the government

Gambling on a cock-fight

contract to carry the royal mails, were a flying symbol of this dashing, scurrying, highly populous society: especially after road surfaces were improved by Telford and Macadam, and the vehicles themselves vastly improved in both comfort and durability. 'Stage-coaches . . . have, combined with the good roads, very much tended to promote that universal intercourse for which Great Britain stands the first in Europe, or on the face of the earth', wrote the author of the *Microcosm* in the first years of the new century. And the English were immensely proud of their road services. Cobbett marvelled at the London–

A stage-coach

Exeter coach doing eight miles an hour over difficult roads. Seven was the average, counting stoppings. Between 1750 and 1830, the time from London to Edinburgh fell from 10 days to 46 hours; from London to Manchester from three days to 18 hours; from London to Bath from two days to 14 hours. Travel at these staggering speeds on the new surfaces in the latest vehicles was already raising humane concern for the well-being of 'the noblest friend of man'. Mr Gray of the *Microcosm* was especially concerned. 'We see frequently from ten to fourteen and even sixteen persons on the top of a stage. . . . The weight of these, together with the vast quantity of luggage stowed in every part, and the massy vehicle capable of supporting such a weight is far too much for four horses at the rate they are forced to go. When we behold four unfortunate animals, too often lame, broken-winded and dreadfully galled by friction, drag along such an immense weight under a burning sun, and suffocated with hot dust. . . . It has been said of England that *she is a paradise for women, a purgatory for servants, and a hell for horses.* The last part of this saying we see most cruelly exemplified here.'

The great coaching era was in full swing with the Regency. The coaching-inns now had their bustling days, maintaining their populations of ostlers, yard-boys, waiters, chamber-maids and boots: the *Bull and Mouth* in Piccadilly, the *White Hart* at Ipswich, the *Angel* at Bury, the *George* in the Borough, *The Elephant and Castle*. . . . The Prince Regent had become

The yard of a large coaching-inn: ostlers and

King George IV before Mr Sam Weller left the *White Hart* for
the personal service of Mr Pickwick; but he, and the bright-eyed
chambermaid, may both be seen to this day haunting the inn-
yard of any coaching-print of the Regency. The achievements of
this, the first, age of speed, however, were confined chiefly to
the great highways. Elsewhere, the old diligence or the
humble stage-waggon, the pack-horse, the post-horse and the
creaking carrier's cart of Mr Barkis remained the common
man's means of travel and transport. Shanks' mare was commonest of all, as it has only ceased to be within living memory.
There was not yet the slightest danger of men losing the use of
their legs. Indeed, the pedestrian feats of ordinary men in the
course of their ordinary business are apt to read like athletic
achievements to a later age. Young Bamford the weaver's boy
from Lancashire, coming back from adventure at sea, thinks
nothing of walking home to Lancashire. From Lancashire to
London and back, at 30 miles a day, begging bread and milk at
farmhouse kitchens and sleeping in hayricks, was the sort of
thing a working-class politician did in the course of duty.
Thomas Holcroft's father 'would often walk to London and
back, more than 60 miles, in the same day'.

Nothing to do with speed, but still a subject for speculation
and wonder, were the new and improved waterways. The
great age of canal-building had opened with James Brindley's
magic feats in the early years of George III's reign. Brindley
was, indeed, among the first of the line of engineers whose
practical skill and ingenuity were to culminate in the great

12

yard-boys loading up coaches at the ' Bull and Mouth'

bridge-building exploits of Smeaton and the Rennies and Brunel, transforming the face of England beyond recognition over the coming century. By the close of the Regency, England was netted in a web of waterways which seemed to have solved the problem of the carriage of heavy imperishable goods. The Regent's Canal Company, in the capital itself, was a late stage of a vast enterprise which had been proceeding for more than half a century. The throngs of navigators who built the canals had already given birth to the navvy, one of the type figures of the industrial age. The ruffians who hatched the Cato Street Conspiracy of 1820 vainly imagined that the navigators of the Regent's Canal might be recruited for their revolutionary purposes. The armies of unskilled workers who carried through the huge enterprises of demolition and reconstruction in

Rolle canal and aqueduct, near Torrington, Devonshire, constructed 1823–4

Regency London heralded the advent of the great labour-gangs that were shortly to build the railways.

Regency England was on the move towards the populous ant-like society of a later age. It was furnishing itself with more and speedier means of movement for both men and materials than England had ever known before. Even steam-driven carriages had put in a brief and frightening appearance on the

Navvies at work on the excavation of the Highgate Archway

roads since Richard Trevithick's first model in 1801. By 1833 steam-coaches were running regularly between London and Brighton, and steam-traction companies were developing the enterprise in the teeth of violent opposition by the vested interests of coaching and early railway companies. They were not finally killed until the 'Man and Flag Act' (limiting road speeds to four miles an hour) in 1864. For all their enthusiasm for progress, the English on the whole preferred the foot-propelled 'hobby-horse'.

Gurney's steam carriage

All the same, the general tempo of life was increasing, and men were proud of the fact, but not yet to the destruction of the amenity of life or the disfigurement of the landscape. The watch, the clock and the calendar were many centuries old, but they had not yet taken charge of men's lives as they were soon to do. Most people still lived their lives to the rhythm of the seasons, although the inhuman rhythm of the machine and the clang of the factory-bell were already impinging on many lives in the industrial districts. Summer time still took priority over a statutory 'Summer Time'.

The survival of the ancient tempo of daily life was reflected in the survival of the meditative trades and professions. The bookseller in a small country town, the stocking-weaver at his frame, the smith at his anvil, the shoemaker at his last—men thus employed had 'time to stand and stare', or even to think. Not that domestic crafts necessarily meant that working life was free and easy. Francis Place, the master breeches-maker of Charing Cross, has told us how work-nausea could afflict the independent craftsman, while Daniel Defoe held that the irregular rhythm of the domestic craftsman had made the English a 'lazy-industrious' folk, alternating between periods of intense industry and drunken stupor or total idleness. Nor need it be imagined that the life, at any rate in urban surroundings, was necessarily quiet. The noise of iron-shod wheels on the stone-setts of city streets was more rather than less shattering than

The craze for hobby-horses

A stocking-weaver

the roll of rubber tyres or the rumble and roar of the internal-combustion engine. The street-cries of hawkers and tradesmen, so dear to the patrons of ye olde worlde, were in their day far more intrusive to the meditative mind than the silent clamour of poster-bills. Even those who lived their lives 'in city pent' —very much a minority of the population—could generally find green fields within easy walking distance, and we know they often did. Most towns had their town-fields where the poorer citizens could find 'Parson Greenfields' on a Sabbath, and despite the progress of enclosure England was still a land of widespread heath and common. The spreading barrier of suburbs and the early manifestations of ribbon-development were still in their infancy. Here, it is true, London was already the great exception. Civil peace and long immunity from foreign invasion had been producing 'London beyond the walls' over several generations. By the early years of the nineteenth century, salubrious areas of suburbia existed at Camberwell and Denmark Hill. In the first year of the Regency, Mr Browning, clerk at the Bank of England, was already living in Camberwell, and in that same year his son, Robert, was born within earshot of nightingales which he believed to embody the souls of Keats and Shelley. By 1823, Mr James Ruskin, sherry merchant, was riding up and down daily between Herne Hill and the City by omnibus, his tall hat under the seat.

A shoemaker

It is safe to say that the average Englishman, if such a term has any meaning, was a countryman, or at any rate a dweller in rural surroundings, even if he got his livelihood only

16

indirectly from the soil, like the village craftsman who might range from Adam Bede to the village blacksmith. Many people still subsisted on locally produced clothes and victuals. Cobbett, returning from a sojourn in America in 1818, professed to have found a great and (in his eyes) a deplorable decline in domestic self-sufficiency. The 'wens' (his favourite name for cities) were devouring market towns and villages, and shops were devouring markets and fairs. 'All was looked for at shops . . . scarcely anyone thought of providing for his own

A streetcryer

wants out of his own land and out of his own domestic means.' He claimed that, when he was a boy (a time round about the 1760s, which he always looked upon with rose-tinted spectacles), 'a manufacturer of shoes, of stockings, of hats, of almost anything that man wanted, could manufacture at home in an obscure hamlet, with cheap house-rent, good air, and plenty of room. . . .' The urbanisation of England was certainly proceeding, slowly but surely; the change that has taken the English from the cottage industries to the super-market.

Something that goes deeper than a change in shopping habits is discernible in the English between Regency and Victorian England. The people of the Regency were the children of a world of highwaymen, outlaws and old rebellion, of savage sports, horseplay and public riot; of a world where every child stood an even chance of dying before the age of five; where the scars of small-pox were accepted as a normal feature of

A village smithy

the human countenance; where parents took their children to public executions for a homily on the wages of sin and to bedlam for amusement. Many a man of the Regency had heard the tale of the 'Forty-five from an aged grandsire before he read Sir Walter Scott. Broadswords as instruments of public policy were still within living memory, and the guillotine a neighbouring rumour. . . . The press-gang, the lash and the gallows were always round the corner.

It was the world of George Borrow, of *Lavengro*, and *The Romany Rye*; of the *Pickwick Papers*, of *Nicholas Nickleby* and *Oliver Twist*. Within half a century of Waterloo it was the England of *Our Mutual Friend*. And after that it may be said to be the England of neither Charles Dickens nor George Borrow but of George Gissing. The late Humphry House in his study of *The Dickens World* put it thus. Between the Pickwick Papers (1837: the year of Victoria's accession) and *Our Mutual Friend* (1865), 'the physique, features and complexions of the characters have changed . . . almost as much as their clothes. . . . We feel that people use knives and forks in a different style . . . the new style is so far developed as to be unmistakable. The people, places, and things become "modern". . . . There is an emotional as well as a practical

The Westminster rat-pit: the celebrated dog Billy killing 100 rats

An edifying spectacle: condemned prisoners being carted off to execution

"consciousness of living in a world of change", an apprehension
of what the changes meant in detail every day, the new quality
of life they brought.' Dickens, the great imaginative genius of
the century, provides us with our most valuable historical
document for this 'new quality of life'. House thought the new
mood and atmosphere were very largely brought about by the
railways, which changed not only the landscape but 'the scope
and tempo of individual living'.

Mr C. S. Lewis would regard as 'the greatest of all divisions
in the history of the West that which divides the present day
from, say, the age of Jane Austen and Scott'. Somewhere
between us and the Waverley Novels, somewhere between us
and *Persuasion*, the chasm runs. He would put this change on a
level with the change from stone to bronze, or from a pastoral
to an agricultural economy. It is epochal. He would say, 'the
greatest change in the history of Western man'. Hereby
Professor Lewis has pin-pointed for us, as near as maybe, the
position of Regency England on the map of history. It is an
era divided from us as by a chasm. It is another world than ours,
disparate, strange, something back beyond the world we know
and in which we live. It is a truly 'historical' era, properly

so-called, and only to be experienced once it has been accepted as such.

Further Reading

John Ashton, *Social Life under the Regency*
E. Beresford Chancellor, *Life in Regency and early Victorian England*
Sir Arthur Bryant, *The Age of Elegance*
William Cobbett, *Progress of a Ploughboy*
William Hazlitt, *Life of William Holcroft*
H. House, *The Dickens World*, Chapter 6
M. Letts, *As the Foreigner saw us*
A Regency Visitor, Prince Pückler-Muskau (Ed. E. M. Butler)
R. J. White, *From Waterloo to Peterloo*

II

The Lower Classes

One of the most immediate impressions that would strike a twentieth-century Englishman, could he be carried back to the England of the Prince Regent, would be the impression of a world in costume. People dressed the part they had to play in life, or at the least displayed some unmistakeable insignia of their craft or calling. It might be (as it still is) a judge's wig or a bishop's lawn sleeves; it might be (as it is no longer) simply a paper cap on the head of a carpenter, or an apron twisted like a sash about the waist of a weaver. It might equally well express a social status, like the merchant's broadcloth and the gentleman's silk cravat. People, especially women, also dressed according to their age. Until very recently the costume of a matron differed greatly from that of a spinster. Hats, too, told a story. By the time of the Peterloo 'massacre' (1819), the white topper had become the head-dress of a Radical leader, serving somewhat the same purpose as Henry IV's white plume at the battle of Ivry ('Watch where you see my white plume shine above the ranks of war!'), and the 'stove-pipe' or the 'chimney-pot' had become the insignia of the City man or the manufacturer by the dawn of the railway age. War, the Powder Tax, and the need to economise in starch and flour had led to the disappearance of powdered wigs, ruffles and frills. It was assumed that loose thinking about the Rights of Man was reflected in the fashion for open-necked shirts, long hair, and trowsers instead of tight pantaloons and knee-breeches. On the whole, it may be said that a more utilitarian style in clothes,

21

Foundry-workers, in knee-breeches

with fewer frills and fripperies, came in with a more industrialised society. Yet it took a long time for a machine-age to iron out all distinctions, and one of the most charming features of engravings depicting industrial scenes is the glimpses they sometimes give us of foundry-men in knee-breeches, and of cocked-hats on the heads of colliers. By 1831, the world was ready for Thomas Carlyle's *Sartor Resartus*, or the Philosophy of Clothes.

The field-labourer in his smock-frock wore the commonest uniform of all, for he was still the commonest figure in the English scene. Even at the mid-point of the nineteenth century, when the census first recorded rural and urban numbers, nearly 50 per cent of English families were living 'under conditions which may properly be classed as rural'. The early years of the nineteenth century were, beyond all question, years of steady depression in the life of the villager. He was fast becoming 'the landless labourer'. The same age which produced the peasant proprietorship of modern France produced the large enclosed farms and highly productive agriculture of early Victorian England. An agricultural revolution had been carried through, agriculture had become a great industry, and England's resources multiplied (some say) twenty-fold. Cobbett remarked upon the dismal fact that 'the labouring *poor*' became a cliché at this time. People no longer talked of 'the labourer' and 'the poor', but now commonly included both in a single phrase to cover the mass of the people who worked on the land. The smock-frock was becoming the badge of a degraded class. Not that the 'chop-sticks', as Cobbett called them, had ever known or expected any but a hard life; nor were they to know any other for long enough yet. The amount of labour available on the land was nearly always in excess of demand. The poverty of the agricultural worker was too often taken to be one of the ineluctable facts of life, or even as evidence of the wisdom of Divine Providence.

The precise condition of the labourer on the land is difficult to recover, for until the nineteenth century the annals of the poor are not merely brief and simple, they are literally non-existent. His memorial is the English landscape, the work of his hands. More personal and particular marks of his sojourn within that landscape are rare indeed. Even his lowly habitations have vanished; scarcely

A farm-labourer

a country cottage in which he lived before Tudor and Stuart times survives. His hovels of thatch and wattle and moistened clay were as ephemeral as the rough habitations of the beasts he tended.

Many labourers lived in the master's farmhouse, marrying late, or not at all, even though breeding. Cobbett blamed the farmer's wife for depopulation of farm-kitchens, for driving the labourers into 'hovels, called cottages', because the once plain and substantial farmhouse had lately developed pretentious items like a 'parlour', a mahogany table, a bell-pull, and a carpet! War-time prosperity when corn-prices were high had much to answer for. . . . The newly genteel lady of the house could not have labourers trampling about on her fine carpets. This, Cobbett observed, was happening in the 1820s. Whatever the cause, labourers were certainly beginning to live out more. Their cottages might be, as Cobbett said, hovels, but they

A farm-labourer's cottage

were more substantial hovels than the long-vanished habitations of their ancestors. The standard English cottage was now of stone, brick or half-timber depending upon the material available in the locality. Similarly with the roofing: thatch, tile or local slate. Windows were glazed, and rarely opened. Privies were rare: middens and the open country were preferred. The amount of accommodation again varied with the locality, the most cribbed, cabined and confined cottages being in areas farthest from the urban centres and the influence of industrial-

A yeoman's farmhouse

ism. In terms of money-wages, again, the labourer's lot was worst in corn-growing areas and in areas farthest removed from urban centres. In Somerset and the south-west a weekly wage of 7s. was common enough long into the Victorian age. Real wages were different, where the labourer had a patch of garden to grow vegetables and keep a pig and poultry, and an employer who allowed him skim-milk, faggots or turf-cutting. In any case, the farm-labourer's lot was a hard one of back-breaking toil, with few and simple pleasures, from earliest childhood to old age. He and his artisan cousin of mine and mill were often called 'the maintaining classes', those who 'are not sought for in public counsel nor . . . found where politic sentences are spoken. It is enough if every one is wise in the working of his own craft: so best will they maintain the state of the world.'

Threshing corn with flails

From little Will Cobbett to Jude the Obscure, with a smock-frock, a piece of bread and bacon, and a bottle of small beer, the labourer on the land went crow-starving at six, graduated to the plough's tail, the pitch-fork and the haywain, and at the close went to sleep with rude forefathers in the churchyard shade. Of such men, a very large part of the world was made and by them it was maintained. Savage oppression was rare; pettifogging injustice—stolen commons, pilfering of cottage-gardens by enclosing landlords, pushing around in the name of charity by squire and parson and their ladies, these were common; worst of all was the stupefying monotony of the daily round and the daily diet. Mechanisation, which can break the monotony of toil and enlist the interest of the young, was slow to develop on English farms, and often violently opposed as a threat to employment. The first successful threshing-machine was used in Scotland at the end of the eighteenth century, and its use spread southward very slowly. The monotony of the farmworker's diet could have been relieved

A plough team

Reaping

if enclosure acts had made proper provision for allotments or cottage-gardens. The labourer's potato-patch was becoming more common in the eighteen-twenties: 'This fashion is certainly a growing one', Cobbett observed. Even the everlasting bread and cheese diet, with the one-day roast meat, was becoming dearer in the period of soaring food-prices during the war-years, and immediately after (1795–1820). Some relief was provided in northern areas by oat-cake, pease-kail, porridge, barley-milk and potatoes. High prices and low wages, together with redundancy in the labour supply after the war, made the labourer's lot particularly hard in the years of the Regency. Where low wages were made up out of the rates—a kind of non-contributory dole system—the labourer suffered by the demoralising effect of subsidised wages upon the wage-rates of the independent labourer. And this, the 'Speenhamland System', lasted from 1795 to 1834.

The depressed status of the wage-labourer on the land should not be confused with the famous phenomenon which is generally known as 'the decline of the yeoman'.

To say the least, the yeoman was more or less always a man of some substance in terms of ownership; of some independence; and with a title that could be defended against any attempt to evict him. While no one could turn him out, he could be squeezed out by competition from stronger men, or tempted to sell out, perhaps by the

The farmworker's diet: beer and cheese

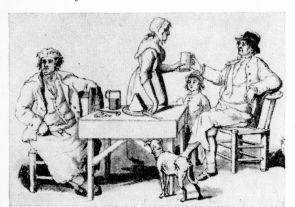

crippling cost of holding his own by law-suits or the heavy expense of fencing his land when enclosure had to be undertaken. He could, and frequently did, lose his footing by speculation in poor land when the price of corn was high and through his inability to redeem his mortgages when prices fell. Taking a base of 100 in 1790, corn prices stood at 187 in 1813, but were down to 113 in 1824. Many small independent farmers borrowed money and invested in marginally profitable cornland at the peak period, when there

A yeoman farmer

was a kind of *terra mania* in some parts of the country. Far from suffering in the peak period on enclosure, the yeoman farmer was often the main beneficiary by it. The sequel is recounted by the Select Committee in 1833: 'In the counties where yeomen heretofore abounded . . . the high prices of the last war led to speculation in the purchase, improvement, and inclosure of land. . . . Prices have fallen, the debt still remains . . . most pernicious to this body of men.'

The celebrated decline of the yeoman, sometimes identified in popular legend with the decline of Old England, was certainly a feature of the Regency and the reign of George IV. He was not the victim of enclosure. He was rather a beneficiary than a victim of the movement which so often injured the small cultivator in the later decades of the eighteenth century. Of him it might be said that, during the war years, he had never had it so good. The prosperous farmer of those years, with his domestic pretentiousness, or what Coleridge called 'the shoal of ostentatious fooleries and sensual vices which the sudden influx of wealth let in on our farmers and yeomanry'—specified by Cobbett in 'bell-pulls and carpets'—was a favourite subject for satire. Cobbett's lament for the decline and fall of the house of Charrington (*Rural Rides*, 20 October 1825) is famous. It was written nearly ten years before the publication of the Select Report on Agriculture, 1833, lending life and concrete

27

'The prosperous farmer . . . with his domestic pretentiousness'

particularity to the generalised conclusions of a parliamentary paper. 'Everything about this farmhouse was formerly the scene of *plain manners* and *plentiful living.* . . . But all appeared to be in a state of decay and nearly of *disuse.* There appeared to have been hardly any *family* in that house, where formerly there were, in all probability, from ten to fifteen men, boys and maids: and, which was worst of all, there was a *parlour.* Aye, and a *carpet* and *bell-pull,* too!'

The place was in the process of being sold up, and Cobbett attended the sale, his heart full of fury and lamentation. He reflected sadly on the good living that had gone on round the good oak kitchen-table, now destined to be bought up by some stock-jobber to be made into the bottom of a bridge over an artificial river in his cockney garden. '"By —— it shan't," said I, almost in a real passion: and so I requested a friend to buy it for me; and if he do so, I will take it to Kensington or to Fleet Street, and keep it for the good it has done in the world.' Anyone inclined to indulge in vague lament over the decline of the yeoman, should first read this vivid valedictory passage in *Rural Rides,* 1825. He should also remind himself that this, and many another sad episode of those years, was a part of the high cost that England paid for the large farms and high farming of early Victorian England.

28

The town labourer thought himself superior to his country cousin, and in wages he was, but he was not as a rule a dis-possessed small-holder who had gone to the town in a desperate search for work and wages. The notion of multitudes flocking to the towns, and from south to north, is a myth. Most of the migrants to the growing towns came from the surrounding countryside and travelled only short distances. There was no serious depopulation of the agricultural districts in the late eighteenth and early nineteenth centuries. What happened often was that demand for industrial labour was met by the natural increase of population that was going on very rapidly at this time, and by the absorption of the unemployed from kindred trades—e.g. handloom-weavers might go into power-loom factories, and lead-miners might turn to coal-mining. There were, and especially when the steam-packet across the Irish Sea provided cheap, one-way tickets, large numbers of Irish immigrants coming into north-western England. 'New' towns were mostly old towns swollen by increasing population, and suffering from over-crowding in consequence. Many men, who had for long enough taken whatever casual work was to hand, were tending to settle down as steady industrial workers simply because there was now a great deal of steady industrial work to be done. The by-industries with which small farmers had for long eked out small agricultural incomes, turning from the plough to the loom or the nail-maker's bench in winter-time, were dying before the advance of larger-scale manufacture. There had been literally hundreds of these half-and-half ways of eking out a subsistence. People who had lived thus, often in rural surroun-dings—truly unclassifiable folk—were tending to settle down into distinct in-dustrial categories of regular employ-ment. Much depended upon the locality, the fertility or otherwise of the soil, the availability of transport and markets.

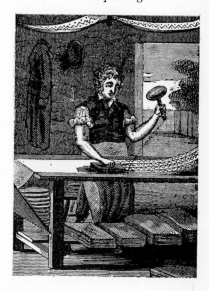

Calico-printing

29

Thomas Howitt, colliery-manager

A family like the Peels, in the neighbourhood of Blackburn, yeomen farmers who had combined weaving with farming, were settling down to calico-printing and spinning-jenny manufacture in the early eighteenth century, and farming was to become increasingly a subsidiary interest. On a lesser scale, Thomas Howitt of Heanor in Derbyshire (father of William, the author), who had combined mine-management with farming, still lived in the comfortable farmhouse, in Regency times, while spending his energy at the coal-pits on the edge of the village. Much the same applies to Thomas Bewick, the engraver's father, at Cherrybourn in Northumberland. Country millwrights and clockmakers found themselves in demand for engineering and tool-making, forming the nucleus of an aristocracy of labour, the civil engineers and mechanics, key-men of the industrial revolution.

The industrial factory-hand, or artisan, was sometimes a man who had deliberately gone to the town from a lowly form of agricultural employment, and, when he was, he seems to have been quite sure that he was bettering himself. The town was the future, a place of opportunity, and—in a delusive sense, perhaps—of freedom. People who sought the opportunities offered by town life may have been deluded, but while it lasted the delusion was a powerful one. The wide-spread and vigorous movement for adult education that was on foot among artisans in industrial centres in the early years of the nineteenth century would suggest that working-men had a good deal more to do than to repine over the lost delights of the village-green. By 1815 there were adult schools in 20 English towns. Brotherly Societies, Artisans' libraries, Bible-reading classes, debating clubs, friendly societies, all and every species of association craft/trade unions are to be found in the urban areas in these years, many of them founded and led by the artisans themselves. Well-disposed persons of superior education, like George Birkbeck, Thomas Hodgskin, Henry Brougham, became patrons and instructors. Self-education was a genuine passion. Working-class politics, coming to life in the years after Waterloo, was largely the offspring of a self-consciousness engendered by an urban environment.

Much depended upon the type of town. An old town, swollen out by new industries and new populations, readily became a slum. Comparatively new towns, largely built to accommodate the increased numbers, might be greatly more tolerable even if they were no less hideous in aspect. Despotic master-manufacturers, like Richard Arkwright at Cromford or Jedediah Strutt at Belper, or Robert Owen at New Lanark, built accommodation for their employees. The buildings might resemble barracks, but they were soundly constructed, very different from the overcrowded hovels where the workmen sought shelter in the purlieus of a medieval city, for businessmen insisted on value for money when they took to building. It would be too much to say that Strutt and Arkwright and Owen were pioneers in workers' flats, but they often put up barracks that possessed the minimum virtues of light and air and elementary sanitation. Every town had its foul courts and alleys, but the really appalling habitations of the back-to-back type, associated with the fell title of 'the Industrial Revolution', were the products of the Victorian age, half a century later. On the whole, the town worker could still indulge some hope of a better future. He was better paid than his country cousin, even if one allows for the difference between money and real wages. Even so, industrial wages—particularly in those trades which

Industrial development: Robert Owen's cotton-mill at New Lanark

were undergoing mechanisation, like those of the handloom weaver—were pitifully small. Worst of all, they were at the mercy of fluctuating markets more acutely than they have ever been since, for self-defence against misfortune was extremely difficult in an age when the most elementary form of union was liable to prosecution under the Combination Acts of 1799–1800. A thriving business like the building trade, with its manifold branches, might mean comparative prosperity for the employee over considerable periods (30–40s. a week in a busy season was not unknown in London by the 1830s: a truly princely rate for that time), but the best paid work was generally at the mercy of seasonal fluctuation.

The typical town-worker of the decade 1820–30, wrote the late Sir John Clapham, after a detailed examination of the situation in these years, 'was not a person who performed for a self-made employer, in steaming air, and with the aid of recently devised mechanism, operations which would have made his grandfather gape'. That situation was still a long way ahead. In fact, the typical town-worker is a lay figure, a faceless abstraction. If the term is to be used at all, it would be safe to say that few town-workers would have submitted to it as a category. Their lives were generally monotonous, dreary, and insecure, but hope springs eternal; and how many poor cotton-spinners or power-loom weavers would have exchanged their lot for that of the slavey below stairs in a London town-house? The female domestics of England were 50 per cent more numerous than the employees in the cotton-trade, and nobody reported on their wrongs until Charles Dickens created 'The Marchioness' and George Moore and Arnold Bennett created Esther Waters and the immortal Elsie. By 1831 there were at least 375,000 male persons engaged in the building trades, about equal to the total in cotton-mills (mostly women and children). England was full

Bricklayers

32

of men, women, and children whose lot was of a middle, or transitional order, betwixt and between cottage and mill; for no single industry had yet passed through a complete technical revolution.

Even in Lancashire, the home of King Cotton, a good deal of spinning was still done by wooden hand-jennies in the 1820s. The self-acting mule of metal construction was only to be found in the more progressive mills. As for weaving, the first steam-loom mill was set up in Manchester in 1806. By 1830 there were

A laundry maid

60,000 power-looms in England and Scotland, but there were still nearly a quarter of a million hand-looms in existence. The hand-loom weaver hung on to a doomed and dying trade until the 'forties, the most pitiable figure in the working population. The domestic worker in textiles, the typical figure in the Lancashire industrial scene at the time of Peterloo (1819), was not the enslaved factory-hand but the craftsman working at a cottage-loom, or frame, even though his machine was hired from a master and his raw material

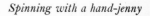

Spinning with a hand-jenny

supplied by him. Dependent for machine, material and market upon a master (quite accurately, an 'entrepreneur'), there was yet an element of freedom and independence in his situation: he could work at his own pace and in his own place. A good many men who worked at home were factory-workers in all but name, and many factory-workers carried an element of craftsmanship and independence into the factory. In the metal-trades, skilled men or 'little masters' often recruited their own labour or employed apprentices in the factory. These factory-apprentices were found in the watch-making trade at Clerkenwell and

33

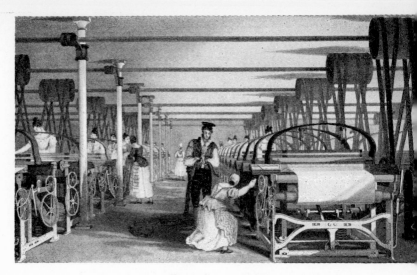

Power-loom weaving

Coventry in 1817. At Abraham Crowley's hardware works in Durham, each master had his own shop in the works, and employed his own labour. How are we to classify the men employed by Mr Copestake of Uttoxeter making artificial jewels? Each man had his own shop in the converted stables around the stable-yard, personally recruiting his own workmen. Similarly, men in the ship-building trade, resenting the notion of their being accounted mere hands, often formed little working-parties which contracted for tasks and rewards with the employers, and a similar contracting system on the part of employees was for long the normal practice in the coal-mines.

Perhaps the colliers were the least classifiable workers in industry. Living as they did in rural settlements where practically everyone was more or less directly engaged in, or dependent upon, a single trade for a livelihood, the colliers were members of a closed community with its own peculiar ways of living and working. Colliers were often regarded as strangers to the larger working community of the country, a race *sui generis*. As late as the 'twenties, an article in the *Penny Cyclopedia* spoke of the colliers of the Black Country coming into the streets of Birmingham like aborigines straying into the urban purlieus of a civilised country, staring about them and stared at, with their black faces and strange speech. Manchester,

too, had its phenomena. In the capital of the cotton trade, there
was something monstrous about the mill employing hundreds of
workers, so monstrous indeed that the cotton-mill was from
the first marked down for state intervention. The first serious
attempt to intervene came in Regency times with the elder
Robert Peel's Factory Act of 1818 to limit the hours of employment of children. But by this time, the recruitment of parish
apprentices to the cotton-mills was on the decline. Even so,
some men were prepared to ridicule the cruel description of
child labour as 'free' labour, and the sanctity of 'freedom of
contract' which involved what Coleridge called 'soul-murder
on the part of the rich and self-slaughter on the part of the poor'.
Yet there were advocates of the factory system as late as 1835
who, like Dr Andrew Ure, likened the labours of factory children
to the sportive dancing of 'lively elves' among the machines,
and could celebrate the blessings of factory industry as 'the
best temporal gift of Providence to the poor'.

We know little at first-hand of the daily life of the factory-
worker of those times, partly because in the earlier phases of
the factory system a very large proportion of the employees
were women and children, and again because their lives of
unremitting and monotonous toil can have yielded little to tell.

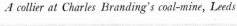

A collier at Charles Branding's coal-mine, Leeds

But we know a good deal about the daily life of the domestic worker because it was at this time that a real live working-man first wrote his memoirs. Perhaps we should say 'of' rather than 'at' this time, for Samuel Bamford composed his *Passages in the Life of a Radical* at the time of the Chartist movement, in the 'thirties and 'forties, and partly by way of offering his somewhat sententious advice to a later generation of Radicals. But Bamford's active years as a working-class politician were precisely those years with which we are here principally concerned, the troubled years between Waterloo and Peterloo, of which latter melancholy affair he left what is our most vivid and valuable account. Bamford was no illiterate newly arrived at a bare literacy. He went to the old Grammar School at his native Middleton, and was never less than handy with his pen. When a working man of loquacious vanity, like Samuel Bamford, arrives at the stage of memoir-writing, he is obviously no longer likely to be a representative working man. All the same, in his verbose *Passages* we have something unique: a weaver's boy speaking out loud and clear from the land of cottage-looms in the industrial heart of Regency England. The domestic worker rather than the factory hand is indeed the typical figure in the textile trades of the Midlands and the North.

Cotton factories in Union Street, Manchester

Factory children

He lived in a cottage of brick and timber, or of timber and daub, beside the village street: a cottage differing little from that of the field-labourer. The floor was a foot or so below the level of the street. The windows were generally larger than those in country cottages in order to afford light for a craft which preeminently required it; indeed, where weaving was undertaken, as distinct from bobbin-winding and auxiliary work of that kind, there might be a special loom-loft, with spacious windows, above stairs. The labours of the domestic worker in textiles, however, were mostly carried on in the main room of the cottage and in the midst of the family, and wives and children generally took their part. The head of the family, dependent on a master for his machine, his warp and weft, and his market, was pace-maker, overseer and guardian. It was his responsibility to maintain safely the valuable piece of plant entrusted to him by the master. When the machine-breakers were about, the master would send out an alarm and offer an advance on the rate for the work, in order to encourage the knitters or weavers to protect the frames. William Felkin, author of the *History of Machine-wrought Hosiery and Lace Manufacture* (1867), remembered riding round the villages on the Notts–Derby border in the winter of 1811, bearing the offer of an advance of a shilling a dozen for the stockingers (of whom his masters employed about three thousand) if their frames were spared destruction. There were dangerous days for the domestic worker in the days of the Luddites.

Bamford was employed in the small tasks of bobbin-winding for his elders from his tenderest years. People, he tells us, made out that religion was a soporific, but he early came to the conclusion that 'there was no religion in the world that could

37

ever make a bobbin-winder content with his lot . . . '. At the same time, he shows us something of the holiday spirit that could lighten the heart of the domestic worker, as distinct from the regimented factory-hand. There was always—weekly, or monthly—'home-bearing day', when the weavers carried their finished work to the master's warehouse, in Manchester, and the boys went with them. Home-bearing day was made into a day out, with all the jollity of trudging along together, with

Cottage industry

numerous calls at the *Hope and Anchor*, the *Flower Pot* and the *Golden Lion*. Here is his portrait of his uncle, a town-weaver in the flesh, setting forth from Middleton: 'He being . . . rather heavy in person would walk rather deliberately, with a stick in his hand, his green woollen apron twisted round his waist, his clean shirt showing at the open breast of his waistcoat, his brown silk handkerchief wrapped round his neck, a quid of tobacco in his mouth, and a broad and rather slouched hat on his head.'

And young Samuel follows behind. 'I with my smaller wallet,

A mill

my rough jacket, my knee-breeches, my strong stockings and
shoes, my open-collared shirt, and pleasure and glee in my heart
and countenance footed the way as lightsomely as a young colt.'

These, with their women-folk, were the men who marched
to St Peter's Fields, Manchester, on that hot August day in
1819, to hear 'Orator' Hunt put the case for the reform of the
House of Commons; 50 or 60 thousand men, women, and
children, dressed in their Sunday clothes, affording—as
Bamford put it—'a display of cleanliness, sobriety and decorum
such as we had never before exhibited'. This great and peaceable

A colliery

rally, which ended in the notorious 'massacre', was no pale-faced proletarian mob, but something more in the nature of an enormous and good-tempered 'home-bearing' of the domestic workers from all the little moorland towns and villages round Manchester. What they were bearing home this time, however, was not 'pollicat' and 'romoll' handkerchiefs, silk and cotton garments from the loom, but the fruit of the political education of a generation.

An 'industrial' market town: Bolton in Lancashire

Bamford's work provides us with a first-hand account, too, of the fun and games, the country customs, the folk-lore and superstitions which enlivened the daily round of dwellers in country places where the clack of the loom mingled with the small sounds of village husbandry, where the ploughboy drove his team within sight and sound of the colliery. England had not yet settled into the universal pattern of Subtopia. How healthful and inspiriting life could be to a boy brought up in that age on the slopes of what D. H. Lawrence, a century later, was to call 'the awful Erewash valley', may be discovered in William Howitt's *Boy's Country Book*, a reminiscence of the early years of the century composed in 1839. Howitt's family came, like Lawrence's, from the little hill-town of Eastwood. It is rare to possess the impressions of two men (both poets, though Howitt was infinitely Lawrence's inferior in this respect) a century apart in time, of life in the self-same small patch of midland earth. For all his life-long love-hatred of that ruined countryside, Lawrence could declare that it still seemed to him extremely beautiful, 'still the old England of the forest and the agricultural past . . . the mines were, in a sense, an accident in the landscape', and life there was 'a curious cross between industrialism and the old agricultural England of Shakespeare and Milton and Fielding and George Eliot . . .'. Howitt's little book, celebrating his boyhood, gives us a vivid record of life before the deluge, so to speak. Like Bamford farther north in Lancashire, he enables us to sense everyday life in Regency England as the ordinary people lived it, with all its strange hybrid quality, far from Nash's London, the Brighton Pavilion, or the polite purlieus of Jane Austen.

English society was a field full of folk, packed with all sorts and conditions of men, women, and children at every stage of transition of a rapidly changing society. When one has accounted for the farm-labourers and the cotton-spinners who stand in the foreground, one looks beyond them to the crowding hordes of domestic servants, blacksmiths, pedlars, and chapmen. A field full of folk, and every one of them, like every one of us, the centre of his own world.

Further Reading

Samuel Bamford, *Passages in the Life of a Radical*
M. Buer, *Health, Wealth & Population, 1760–1815*
A. E. Dobb, *Education and Social Movements*
R. S. Fitton and A. P. Wadsworth, *The Strutts and the Arkwrights*
M. George, *The Age of Transition*
J. L. and B. Hammond, *The Town Labourer*
— —, *The Village Labourer*
William Howitt, *The Boy's Country Book*
Andrew Ure, *The Philosophy of Manufacture* (*1835*)
F. Podmore, *Robert Owen*

III

The Middle
and Upper Classes

The 'maintaining classes', the great multitude who maintained
the state of the world, were not traditionally part of the political
state. They did not as yet enjoy (as the phrase goes) a 'constitutional presence', but were represented in the politics of
the nation by their attachment to one or another of the great
interests which were represented in the legislature. As William
Paley expressed it: 'We have a House of Commons composed
of 540 members, in which number are to be found the most
considerable landholders and merchants of the kingdom; the
heads of the army, the navy and the law; the occupiers of the
great offices of state; together with many private individuals
eminent for their knowledge, eloquence, or activity. Now if the
country be not safe in such hands, in whose may we confide its
interests? . . . The different *interests* are actually represented,
and of course the people *virtually*.'

The term 'the people', as Disraeli insisted as late as 1834 in
The Spirit of Whiggism, was not a political term, but a term of
natural history. Shelley, writing his *Philosophic View of Reform*
in 1819–20, however, had pointed out that 'Virtual Representa-
tion' of the common people had ceased to be a valid argument,
for a Fourth Class had now made its appearance in the nation,
the unrepresented multitude. The nation had become multiplied
into a denomination which had no constitutional presence in the
state, a denomination whose interests had previously been
'sensibly interwoven with that of those who enjoyed a constitutional presence', but were so no longer. The mass of the
people, in fact, was becoming a properly political term.

Edmund Burke had given expression to the older view, in 1796: 'Those who, in any *political* view, are to be called the people, are of adult age, not declining in life, of tolerable leisure for such discussions, and of some means of information, above menial dependence: i.e. about 400,000. This is the British public; and it is a public very numerous. The rest, when feeble, are the objects of protection; when strong, the means of force.' 'The rest', were generally called the 'mobility', or the 'multitude', or even (by Burke in a deplorable moment) the 'swinish multitude'. Even a supposedly left-wing document of the Commonwealth in the seventeenth century, made it clear under the title of *The agreement of the People,* that 'the people'—so far as franchise was concerned—meant householders, payers of the poor-rate, and excluded servants and people in receipt of wages. Despite the American and the French Revolutions, traditional opinion in England in the early years of the nineteenth century still meant by 'the people', in any political view, ratepayers and householders: in short, the lower middle class, and upward.

This body of persons, the public or the political people, was—as Burke said—a very numerous body, and of extremely mixed and variegated composition. The bulk of it consisted of 'the middle classes', a phrase always to be most meticulously used in the plural, for in England there have always been many shades and grades of 'middle'. At the time with which we are here concerned, England was the commercial nation *par excellence*, pervaded with the habits and standards of business from top to bottom. Since this was the most successful nation in the cultivation of trade and industry, her middle classes had a universality, a representative character, a ubiquity, which called forth foreign envy and domestic satire as never before or since. 'The nation of shopkeepers' was a term of envious contempt to Napoleon, and

A merchant

a perfectly accurate and laudatory description with Adam Smith. When, in 1814, the painters, Haydon and Wilkie, visited the Louvre, Haydon asked his companion how he would identify the English among the crowds thronging the galleries. Wilkie 'looked a minute, and contemplating their sedate, respectable, monied look by the side of the Russians and French, said: "Dear, dear, they just look as if they had a balance at their bankers."' Europe in general knew the

Commercial England: St Katherine's Docks, London

Englishman with his long purse, his insular manners, and his comfortable self-esteem. He had never looked more himself than in the present hour, and as the century went on the satirical gaze of Europe hardened into savage contempt on the faces of domestic observers. The hell of the English, Carlyle announced, is the hell of unsuccess. The refrain from Arthur Clough's *Dipsychus* (1862) '*It's nice to have money . . .*' was the signature-tune of the English for several generations before it was written down. Coleridge, perhaps the most profound social critic of the Regency, produced his *Lay Sermon* in 1817, attributing all his country's unhealth to 'the *overbalance* of the commercial spirit'.

The middle classes were not exclusively composed of business men, merchants, traders, and shopkeepers. They included the professional men, officers of the armed forces, parsons, lawyers, doctors, and dons, men who practised some science or who lived on some intellectual stock-in-trade, 'the clerisy' as

Coleridge called them, or, in a less attractive modern phrase, the intelligentsia. These men and their ladies composed, for the most part, the attractive provincial world of Jane Austen. Their peculiar snobbery was their aloofness from trade and their fringe relationship with the aristocracy. They were not aloof from the 'deserving' poor, with whom—especially if they belonged to the parsonage—they had what might be called a 'coal-and-blanket' relationship. They also formed the bulk of the reading public, patronising the circulating libraries and the booksellers. The notion that the English middle classes were largely philistine is a transposition of a later state of things into an earlier age. Of course, there was always the *nouveau riche* man of business who bought books by the yard to display behind glass for social prestige. But the middle classes of the early nineteenth century were for the most part decently educated and of a decent respect for culture. Very many persons in these parts of society were Dissenters, excluded (by their own

A prosperous middle-class family

choice rather than by the law, at this time) from the ancient schools and universities. The well-to-do Dissenters formed almost a second world of their own, aloof from the traditional institutions of the aristocracy. They had their own academies where their

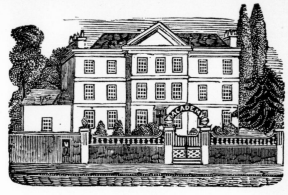

An academy

sons acquired a type of education which we should call modern when compared with the classical education purveyed by the older academic bodies. They prized geography, history, the sciences, modern languages, studies which meant more to business folk than Latin and Greek, Hebrew, Divinity, and moral philosophy. Learning, like everything else, was to be appraised in terms of its utility. This was not philistine at any higher level than Thomas Gradgrind's academy. Combined with evangelical religion, it helped to make the middle class of business the source of much that was liberal and humane in the great age of industrial and commercial expansion on the eve of Victorian England.

If the middle classes were often smug, purse-proud and snobbish, it is well to remember that these have been characteristic of lately successful well-to-do people in all ages. It is certainly true that the middle classes were particularly pleased with themselves at this time. Some of their self-conceit may well have been the compensatory reaction of a class which felt itself to be misprized politically. Very few men of business had any place in the political establishment at that time. When the parliamentary franchise was slightly extended in 1832, many members of the shopkeeper class found themselves brought for the first time within the pale of the constitution. The £10 householder was the advance-guard of universal suffrage. Of course, mercantile wealth found many indirect means of making itself felt in the nation's politics, but the holders of such wealth, great or small, merchants or shopkeepers, justly felt that their constitutional presence hardly reflected their social and economic importance. Bitterly, contemptuously, they expressed their resentment in scornful allusion to 'aristocratic triflers'. Solemnly, portentously, they made known their pride and joy in middle-class worth. . . . 'Let the grandees have their learned playthings', wrote Andrew Ure in his exultant treatise on *The Philosophy of Manufactures* (1835); 'they may be allowed freely to waste their early years in the pastime of

The Burlington Arcade

scanning Greek and Roman metres, provided they do not fancy themselves thereby, albeit ignorant of the principles of Science, Art, and Trade, qualified to scan the measures and to regulate the affairs of empires at their will.' *The Westminster Review*, the philosophic-radical journal, assured the middle classes in 1826 (as if they needed any assurance) that the whole world acknowledged their growing numbers and importance. 'These classes have long been spoken of, and not grudgingly by their superiors themselves, as the glory of England; and that which alone gives us our eminence among nations; as that portion of our people to whom everything that is good among us may with certainty be traced.'

Moreover, they were the cement of society, the best guarantors of social peace. What mattered an occasional disturbance in a manufacturing district where there was an unhappy deficiency of the middle rank, where the children of the poor lacked the good example of middle-class families to look up to? Fortunately, James Mill congratulated his countrymen, 'there can be no doubt that the middle rank, which gives to science, art, and to legislation, their most distinguished ornaments, the chief

A linen-draper's shop

source of all that has exalted and refined human nature', is the rank which will always guide and direct the rest. The opinions of the people below the middle rank are formed and directed 'by that intelligent and virtuous rank who come the most immediately in contact with them . . . to whom they fly for advice and assistance in all their numerous difficulties . . . in health and sickness, in infancy and in old age; to whom their children look up as models . . . whose opinions they hear daily repeated, and account it their honour to adopt.' Mill, at that time (he was writing in 1819, the year of Peterloo!) was probably right. The alliance between middle and working class, although often uneasy, and eventually regretted, was crucial to the achievement of the slender measure of parliamentary reform that was achieved in 1832. More important still, the alliance contributed much to the peaceable outcome of a struggle that contained many elements of bitterness.

As for the contest between a commercial middle-class and a landed aristocracy, although the language of the time would sometimes suggest that it was conscious, sharp, and vengeful, it was largely a myth, a matter of gusty battle-cries, pulled punches, shadow-boxing and frequent fraternisation. For there

49

was no hard and fast line between merchant and country gentleman. The gentleman very often drew a goodly proportion of
his income from investment in trade and manufacture, and
the merchant was ready to invest in land, not only because
it was the safest form of investment but also because landed
property was the surest source of social prestige and political
influence. Mutual animosities were far more often fomented by
interested parties than the outcome of real social forces. The
value of a wealthy country gentleman of old family, like Sir
Francis Burdett, to the Radical cause was immeasurable in the
post-war years; the baronet, as Cobbett said, was the most
influential and popular man in England with 'the really efficient
part of the people'. Next to Burdett, Henry Hunt ('Orator'
Hunt) drew the biggest crowds, and Hunt might have been a
conscious parody of Burdett, tails, topper, fine linen, topped-
boots and all. The Orator was no gentleman, but it was no small
part of his political stock-in-trade to look like one. He was, in
fact, what in Ireland they called a 'squireen'. He rode furiously
to hounds, and he took his political fences in the same
fashion.

The Regency saw the English country gentleman in the
fine flower of his genius as a social type.

Dressed for the country

Indeed, it was at this time that he became
a standard model for the English 'gentleman' in general. His clothes, under the
jurisdiction of Beau Brummell, became a
kind of uniform which English gentlemen
wore with remarkable rigidity for more
than a century. They were outdoor clothes,
the tailed riding-coat, double-breasted, the
white linen stock wound about the throat
and tied in a bulky bow, the tall hat with
a curly brim to serve as a crash-helmet,
tight breeches and riding-boots which required only to be loosened in order to
become trousers. They were the country
clothes of the country gentleman, the an-
cestor of the Englishman's 'sports clothes',

50

and every man who has worn them since that time has had somewhere within him the vestigial remains of 'squire'— even if no more than a hankering after the weekend cottage, or hacking about the roads on a hired nag on a Saturday afternoon or a Sunday morning. It was in Regency

The country gentleman

England—at any rate within the life-time of George IV—that the pattern was set, sartorially, and ever since he has been seen everywhere, the more or less perfected model of the country gentleman. Variants and versions of him are to be seen in John Bull, Mr Pickwick and Johnny Walker—still going strong.

The great original, the admired type, was perhaps the most remarkable species that England has ever produced. The country gentleman was remarkable because he was a gentle-man, in the sense of being a man of breeding, and a countryman in the literal sense of belonging to the land. The essence of him was celebrated in Wilfrid Scawen Blunt's *The Old Squire.*

> *I like the hunting of the hare*
> *   Better than that of the fox . . .*

> *Nor has the world a better thing,*
> *   Though one should search it round,*
> *Than thus to live one's own sole king,*
> *   Upon one's own sole ground.*

> *I leave my neighbours to their thought;*
> *   My choice it is, and pride,*
> *On my own lands to find my sport,*
> *   In my own fields to ride.*

*The hare herself no better loves
  The field where she was bred
Than I the habit of these groves,
  My own inherited.*

Shooting

His roots were in the soil as firmly and inextricably as those of any day labourer; more so, since squire had his title-deeds and wasn't to be turned out, while humbler figures in the landscape could be, and often were. He lived where most of England lived: in market town and village and hamlet. He governed a great deal of England, too, from the Bench as Justice of the Peace and from the saddle as Captain of Yeomanry. The people of the land depended upon him for their cottages, for their rough justice, for their relief in poverty, for their daily livelihood. Upon his personality often depended whether their lives were tolerable or miserable; both the strength and the weakness of the ancient system of government which centred

'The savage enforcer of the Game Laws'

in the unpaid magistracy lay in this, its capriciously personal character. On the one hand, squire might be renowned mainly as the savage enforcer of the Game Laws; on the other he might be, like Sir Robert Heron, the Lincolnshire patriarch who, in the lean year of 1814, ensured garden and pasture for one cow for all his labourers, while his lady employed the women 'of decent character' in 'our four villages' in spinning. He might be an unkempt brute like Sir Pitt Crawley, a poltroon like Festus Derriman, or a great 'improving' gentleman of the soil like Thomas Coke of Holkham. He might be a Nimrod like Jack Mitton, or a bruiser like Jack Musters, or a scholar-squire who never missed a mill with bare fists like Windham of Felbrigg.

'Humane man-trap' (*From an ironfounder's catalogue*)

Whatever his beliefs—and he might be a Tory die-hard like Lord Redesdale or a Radical like Sir Francis Burdett—one thing he could always be depended on to be: a sporting animal. Scholarly or half-illiterate, he took it for a matter beyond argument that his order existed to hunt and shoot and raise the price of corn. More especially to hunt the fox. He was capable of raising fox-hunting to the status of a primary principle of national well-being. Sir John Eardley-Wilmot, in his *Reminiscences of Thomas Assheton-Smith*, the celebrated fox-hunting M.P., assures us: 'The manly amusement of fox-hunting is the best corrective to those habits of luxury and those concomitants of wealth which would other-wise render our aristocracy effeminate and degenerate; it serves to retain the moral influence of the higher over the lower classes of society, and is one of the strongest preservatives of that national spirit by which we are led to cherish above all things a life of active energy, independence and freedom.

The National sport: hunting

> *' Thus trained, my masters, you would meet the foe,*
> *Furious to battle as to covert go.*
> *A cavalry already formed the French to rout,*
> *And " Tally-ho!" your frantic war-whoop shout!'*

Little wonder that a pack of hounds went with Wellington to
the Peninsula.

At all times of rapid social change on the English countryside
we come upon a great deal of indignant outcry against an
upstart gentry which is said to be displacing 'the good old
aristocracy'; moneyed men from the town, profiteers, usurers,
nabobs, stock-jobbers and pensioners, buying up the estates
of the old, native gentry. In the years which followed upon
the close of the Napoleonic Wars, this kind of outcry was
particularly rife, and the foremost voice in vituperation was of
course that of William Cobbett. Year after year, in page after
page of furious invective, Cobbett declaimed against 'the new
gentry', the lickspittle lords from 'Change Alley' and Lombard
Street, sometimes sons of Moses, who were supplanting the
true native gentlemen of England. The man is a shallow fool
who cannot duly estimate the difference between 'a resident
native gentry, attached to the soil, known to every farmer and
labourer from their childhood, frequently mixing with them in

those pursuits where all artificial distinctions are lost, practising hospitality without ceremony, from habit and not on calculation; and a gentry only now-and-then-residing at all, having no relish for country delights, foreign in their manners, distant and haughty in their behaviour, looking to the soil only for its rents, viewing it as a mere object of speculation, unacquainted with its cultivators, despising them and their pursuits, and relying for influence not upon the goodwill of the vicinage, but upon the dread of their power.' It was all the fault of Mr Pitt and paper-money. 'The war and paper-system has brought in nabobs, negro-drivers, governors, admirals, generals, loan-jobbers . . . contractors . . . pensioners . . . bankers . . . stock-jobbers. . . .'

The social change brought war to the countryside, for, whenever any of the new men went to the country, as Cobbett declared, 'they looked upon it that they were to begin a sort of warfare against everything around them'. Not the least of their defects was their beastly lack of taste. When you came upon a country house that looked like a sort of church, in a somewhat Gothic style of building, with crosses on the tops of different parts of the pile, made out of bits of Scotch fir nailed together, you might be sure that the place belonged to some honest person from the 'Change or its neighbourhood. 'Not a bad plan', Cobbett recommended, for 'fundlords who retire to be country-squires'. A good way to show the antiquity of their origins. 'Such fooleries I never before beheld.' This is at any rate one interpretation of the gothic revival, which constituted one feature of the Regency landscape. Cobbett, the 'ranting Radical', hated the bogus and the pretentious. That he hated and distrusted the class which held a monopoly of power in the countryside is only true with a distinction. Shelley, who came of that class, made the same distinction when he recommended distinguishing between 'the Corinthian capital of polished society, and the creeping weeds which deface the rich tracery of its sculpture'. Looking back at the end of his life, Cobbett disclaimed all disrespect for persons of rank and station, but he thought that 'the present Lords differed from the Lords of former times . . . in everything; except the shape

Rebuilding à la mode

of their bodies', and that nobility had given way to 'a prodigious band of spungers living upon the labour of the industrious part of the community'.

The nobility was originally called 'the Corinthian capital of polished society' by Edmund Burke. It was part of the old snob's apologia for the ancien régime. So far as Regency England was concerned, it was more often than not a case of misapplied epithet. The nobility in England like every other class, were a mixed crowd. 'There is nothing like 'em when they add intelligence to breeding', Haydon noted after a visit to Lord Egremont at Petworth. If he had paid a visit to Holkham Hall for one of Mr Coke's 'clippings', he might have sat down with the Norfolk farmers, where 'the smallest tenant farmer was given as ready a hearing as any of the great territorial magnates who regularly attended'. Had he visited the Duke of Bridgwater, he would have found the Canal Duke talking broad Derbyshire under the influence of Jim Brindley, the magical millwright. Blood was never ennobled in England, and the nobility was never an isolated and exclusive caste. The younger sons and brothers of noblemen were commoners and frequently engaged in trade or lived as plain country gentlemen, though it is true that a peer more often mis-married with an actress than with a tradesman's daughter. There were idle and merely decorative noblemen in plenty, but it was more typical of a peer to live on his estates and set up as an improving landlord, or a dabbler in the stock-market. The important thing about him is that the English peerage was never a merely *fainéant* class. Its members belonged to the real and constructive activities of society. Much that they did may have appeared frivolous, selfish, even harmful. But few would have qualified for the fate which overtook the useless aristocracies of Continental Europe. Long into the nineteenth century, for better or for worse, the aristocracy great and small were very much responsible for the way things went in England.

The line of social demarcation between the upper and the lower aristocracy was probably the sharpest in English society. Jane Austen certainly found it so; indeed, took it for granted. The good society of her novels was that of the county families, squires and parsons and professional men and officers of the Services. Mr Darcy was vaguely connected with the peerage, but Miss Elliot, who 'had been walking after Lady Russell out of all the dining-rooms and drawing-rooms in the county' for years, did not expect to dine in a nobleman's house. Baronets

Afternoon tea

The Devonshire minuet

were frequent, but lords were only to be seen occasionally, and distantly, at a county ball or an assembly. Lord Portsmouth, who lived in the Rev. Mr Austen's household as a pupil, was well known to be a fool and an eccentric. Otherwise, never a Peer in sight. At the other end of society were the Bigg Walkers and the Digweeds who *rented* the manor-house at Steventon. They provided comic-relief as gentry. As for the yeomen-farmers, oh dear no! 'The yeomanry,' Emma declares firmly, 'they are precisely the order of people with whom I feel I can have nothing to do.' Poor Harriet must be told that she 'would throw herself out of all good society' were she to marry that decent good-natured farmer, Bob Martin, and Harriet agrees that 'he is not so genteel as a real gentleman'. The less caste there is about a society, it seems, the more snobbery. This was especially true about Regency England, when pressure upwards from newly moneyed claimants to the *entrée* was strong and constant. Jane Austen was infallible in such matters. Her refinements upon the grades of gentility are scarcely surpassed by the most exquisite social analysts of China. Nor are her observations entirely the deliverances of irony and humour, as may be gathered by comparing her letters with her novels. 'She has', as Sir Harold Nicolson has said, 'provided posterity with an incomparable analysis of English upper-middle and lower-middle society at the time of the Industrial Revolution.' We might rather say of Regency England, for it was of those years, and in those years,

A musical evening

that her finest work was done. 'The type of civility she depicts', Sir Harold concludes, 'was undistinguished, heartless and base.'

Heartless and often mean that society might be, but it was saved from the worst perils of social collision by certain ameliorative forces in the social scene. 'The classes of our social fabric have, here and there, slight connecting links, and provincial balls are one of these' wrote George Meredith, in *Evan Harrington*. Here, the son of a half-pay captain, or of a retired tea-merchant, or of a village doctor, or even of a masquerading lord, might 'fall victim of Cupid's levelling dart'. There is to be remembered, too, the infinitely complicated and widely distributed middle which linked the extremes of English society. In this infinitely complex area, did anyone, even Jane Austen, know precisely where a trade left off and a profession

Officer and Gentleman

began? Of course, everyone knew, as Robert Southey observed at the outset of his career, that, if one was cut out from a commission in the armed forces by one's pacifist principles, one was left only with the church and the bar. But who could be quite sure about a *dentist*? On the one hand there was the horse-doctor who pulled teeth at a shilling a time. On the other there was Mr Cartwright, the fashionable practitioner, who—as

Prince Pückler-Muskau recorded—'makes £10,000 a year and goes to no one except the King. *C'est un Grand Seigneur dentiste*. . . .' Even the doctor might vary from the old friend of Samuel Bamford, 'Doctor' Healey, a village herbalist and 'pothecary who supposed that he got into the surgical profession by deriving a taste for it from his father, to the fashionable Doctor Addington, father of the Home Secretary, Viscount

A physician

59

A clergyman of the Establishment

Sidmouth. Everyone knew that a clergyman of the Established Church, let his appearance and his poverty be what they may, 'is always treated as a gentleman, and is entitled by right of his sacred office to be admitted, and is received, into the best company upon a footing of equality'. But what of the writer of these words, in somewhat embittered mood, the Rev. William Jay, Evangelical preacher? What of the myriad Dissenting preachers up and down the land? Was the social standing of the Rev. Patrick Prunty and the Rev. George Austen determined simply by the fact that the one had his parish in Yorkshire and the other had his two livings in Hampshire? On the other hand, the phrase 'an officer and a gentleman' was both euphonious and accurate in everyone's ears. The daughters of the Great Mel, the tailor who never sent in a bill, were quite indifferent whether their brother, Evan Harrington, became an officer in the Army or in the Navy, 'as long as they could win for their brother the badge of *one* Service, "when he is a gentleman at once"'! Moreover, it was always up to the son of a coal-heaver to prove himself as good a man as the son of a belted earl with his bare fists without being set upon by the gentleman's lackeys in the manner that happened to François-Marie Arouet when he bit his thumb at the Chavalier de Rohan in Paris. The annals of sport, more especially of pugilism, afford some highly instructive lessons in the dissolvents of class-barriers in the age of the great bruisers and the Corinthians. Field-sports and farming, and even religion, are not unprofitable areas of research in this matter. Hazlitt's *On going to a fight*, and certain chapters in Borrow's *Lavengro*, should always stand high in the social bibliography of the Regency, close behind Miss Austen's novels and that most comprehensive mirror of the age, *Vanity Fair*.

Further Reading

R. W. Chapman, *Jane Austen, facts and problems*
Lord David Cecil, *The Young Melbourne*
Mrs George Grote, *Life of George Grote*
E. Inglis-Jones, *The Great Maria*
G. E. Milton, *Jane Austen and her times*
H. Nicolson, *Good Behaviour*
A Regency Visitor, Prince Pückler-Muskau (Ed. E. M. Butler)

IV

London

This city now doth, like a garment, wear
The beauty of the morning; silent, bare,
Ships, towers, domes, theatres and temples lie
Open unto the fields, and to the sky;
All bright and glittering in the smokeless air . . .

William Wordsworth must have got up very early in the morning of that summer day in 1802; before the citizens had lighted their fires. London had been notorious for two centuries and more for the sea-coal smoke from the thousands of domestic hearths, lying low upon its thoroughfares. Wordsworth wrote his sonnet on Westminster Bridge 10 years before the official opening of the Regency, and nearer 20 years before John Nash's attempt to make the Regent's capital a place of imperial majesty. The City sky-line was still the sky-line of Sir Christopher Wren, dominated by the white silhouette of the ancient Tower, the soaring dome and golden cross of St Paul's, and the pinnacles of the City churches. The whole panorama bore the tint of warm red-brick. It was still the London that Canaletto had painted in the 1760s. The bridge on which Wordsworth stood, however, was a landmark in the transformation of medieval London into a modern city. Westminster Bridge may be said to have founded the great English tradition of bridge-building that was to go on with Smeaton, and Telford, and the Rennies, even though its builder was a Swiss. Charles Labelye had built it, and it was promoted by the ninth

62

The City sky-line, from Blackfriars Bridge

Earl of Pembroke. It was under construction from 1739 to 1750, and it cost nearly £400,000. It was to stand until 1861. Wordsworth had the great city of the future, if not before his eyes, at least beneath his feet.

To Cobbett, London was always 'the Great Wen'. To Samuel Bamford, the Lancashire weaver who visited it in the winter of 1816–17, it was 'the great Babylon'. Not a word does either of them have to say of the splendid transformation that was under way at that time beneath the hand of the Regent and his architects. They seem to have seen only London's enormity. It is true that it was growing rapidly. It had a population of well over a million by 1811, and was spreading its tentacles like an octopus. But then, London had always been by far the greatest centre of wealth and population in the king's dominion. Of late it had been swallowing up large areas of its own suburban circumference, while its tendency to attract to itself the energy and talent of the country at large had lately become more marked than ever. In the eighteenth century, such places

63

as Birmingham, Norwich, Bristol, and Derby had enjoyed a vigorous intellectual life of their own, not to mention the claims of Edinburgh to be the Athens of the North. There was Erasmus Darwin and the Lunar Society in the Birmingham area. Norwich had its Aldersons, Taylors, Smiths, and Martineaus, and the Norwich School of painting was to linger there for several generations yet. There was once a Wright of Derby, a genius who lived and painted and was buried in his county town, and who is still remembered by the name of his native city. But no one would ever dream of speaking of Reynolds of Plympton, or Lawrence of Devizes, or Gains-borough of Sudbury, who were all displaced provincials absorbed by London. Benjamin Robert Haydon, the most grandiose historical painter of the Regency, came up from Plymouth in 1804 with his head stuck out of the window of the London coach, gaping for the first sight of St Paul's. London, 'where the streets are paved with gold', drew provincial genius irresistibly, draining provincial society of its once vigorous elements like a syphon. In the early years of the new century, there was even a Cockney School of Poetry. The imperial capital, the seat of government, the heart of the financial colossus, the throne of Mars, was becoming the heart and seat and throne of the nation's energies more certainly than ever before. It was, the Prince Regent decided, worthy of an architectural splendour to rival that of Rome itself.

It was fortunate that the architectural rehabilitation of London came when it did, and that it was undertaken by men who were not afraid of bold enterprise, visionary planning, and financial risk. These qualities would have been disastrous had they not also been men of taste. They came at a time when architectural standards in England were higher—at least as regards urban building—than they had ever been, and perhaps were ever to be again. For England lacked a great urban tradition. Manor house and parish church had for centuries monopolised the architectural genius of the nation. Except, as at Blandford Forum in Dorset, where fire had cleared a site, it was their habit to allow their towns to proliferate like rabbit-warrens around some ancient monument of a castle or a cathedral. Now, at last, the English were to match their older glories in domestic architecture, with an urban style second to none. Such a style had been showing itself for a century before the Regent and John Nash entered upon the scene. Georgian England was the forefather of Regency England. Indeed, it is possible to hold the view that the Regency ruined a native

The Egyptian Hall, Piccadilly, designed by P. F. Robinson, 1812

tradition of grace and moderation, imposing upon it an otiose and extravagant pastiche, part Classic, part Gothic, with an admixture of Egyptian and Oriental, liberally tarted up with the picturesque: a composite which is the negation of a style. And there is indeed something monstrous about the works of the Regency. Turning the boastful pages of *Metropolitan Improvements* (1827), it is a little difficult to avoid a whiff of nausea as the grandiose scenes unfold. Everything is so big, so

The Coliseum, Regent's Park, designed by Decimus Burton

bold, so elephantine with marching columns and colonnades, so oppressive with sculptured pediments, so pretentious in orders and ornament. We ask, where are the blazing blue skies of Italy and Greece that could control such monuments in other days and other climes? These immensities might be expected to look as ludicrous as soaking togas under London fog and rain. Gleaming stone and stucco might be expected to blacken into shabby pretentiousness beneath the sullying touch of city smoke.

Visiting London in the year of the Prince's death (1830, when he was King George IV), Maria Edgeworth was already striking the note of doom. She was 'properly surprised by the new town that has been built in the Regent's Park—and indignant at plaister statues and horrid useless *domes* and pediments crowded with mock sculpture figures which damp and smoke must destroy in a season or two.' She would concede that 'some of the plaister streets are really magnificent when one forgets that they are plaister. But', she concluded, 'there is ever some voice which cries Must fall! Must fall! Must fall! Must scale off—soon, soon, soon.'

Regency London, however, was brash and boastful, shouting
defiance at the memory of Nineveh and Tyre. It was celebrating
not only the brief reign of the first Prince of Taste since
Charles I, but the exuberant mood of a nation which thought
itself to have much to be proud of. Its bold façades and sweeping
vistas celebrated victory even before victory had been won.
Napoleon had yet to set out for Moscow, and the Duke had
yet to drive the French from Spain, when the Prince set John
Nash to his imperial exploits. The hour and the man had come
together. It was in 1811 that Marylebone Park reverted to the
Crown, releasing several hundred acres for development north
of the New Road (now the Marylebone Road). Various schemes
had been prepared for the exploitation of this accession of
crown land. If it were to attract fashionable London northward
it would have to be laid out with suitable grace and dignity. This
might have been achieved adequately, if without originality, by
extending the style of Bloomsbury—the grid pattern of streets
and squares. Nash proposed instead an aristocratic garden-city,
an elegant composition of terraces, groves, and free-standing
villas. In fact, old Marylebone Park should become the Regent's
Park, replete with a guingette—a royal pleasure-house—a

A villa in the Regent's Park: Grove House

double circus, to outshine anything at Bath, ornamental lakes and waterways, terraces, bosky groves, and private residences to rival the hotels of Paris. Indeed, the Prince (who was to suffer from a fantasy that he had personally assisted at Waterloo) talked much of putting Napoleon's Paris in the shade with charms and splendours appropriate to the capital city of the first gentleman presiding over the top nation.

The Regent's Park, however, was only the northernmost limit of Nash's design. If it were to house top people, it must be suitably linked with Westminster and Whitehall, the seat of government, and with Carlton House, the seat of the Prince. For this purpose, Nash planned a great metropolitan thoroughfare, Regent Street, to drive north and south between the Regent's Park and St James's Park. This was Nash's 'Royal Mile', built between 1817 and 1823, with its noble Quadrant to solve the problem of the kink northward of Piccadilly, and its panoramic vistas closed to the north of Oxford Circus by the spire and vestibule of All Souls, Langham Place, and the Corinthian portico of the Haymarket theatre. Nash's plan included also a working-class quarter to the east of the Regent's Park, complete with market and shops and a canal-basin served from the Regent's Canal fringing the north and north-east

Middle-class homes in Park Village East, Regent's Park

The Quadrant, Regent Street, designed by John Nash, 1819–20

borders of the Park itself. He also planned to treat St James's Park on the same principles as the Regent's Park, in order to make a pair, north and south. In the middle of the 1820s he was planning to link up both Whitehall and Regent Street with Bloomsbury, the central feature being a large square at the top of Whitehall (Trafalgar Square had to wait until 1836), rebuilding much of the rather squalid property around St Martin's. Hardly any of the buildings in these areas were designed by Nash. Cubitt, Wilkins, Smirke and others were responsible for most of them; John Nash was but one bright and dramatic star in the galaxy of architectural talent that graced the urban sky in this age of transformation.

John Nash might best be called the politician and the business manager of this great scene. He was the man who had the confidence of the Prince who had his fingers on the purse-strings. He would make his sketches of detail and hand them out to others; sometimes they came off, sometimes they did not. The result might be superb, a *grand coup d'oeil* which still enchants the eye and staggers the imagination with illusions of grandeur. On closer inspection the thing might well affront the conscience with suspicions of the slap-dash, the super-ficially impressive, even the shoddy. Behind the glory of the terraced front might stand gimcrack segments of domestic interior like stale sandwiches in a beautiful box, although it must be said that Nash was a great stickler for domestic amenities, sound ventilation, heating, plumbing and 'all modern comforts . . .'. The smooth and handsome coats of stucco might quickly flake and crack, but such is the nature of stucco. Probably he would not have minded the jibe: 'he found London brick, and he left it stucco'. For he was above everything a man who courted the fashion, and fully shared the grandiloquent, not to say exuberant, mood of his age. Like his near contemporary, the Rev. Sydney Smith, he would cheerfully have asked: why should I do anything for posterity? What has posterity done for me? He was not building for posterity. He was building for the Prince Regent, and incidentally for John Nash. He made a good thing of his trade.

Nash was a business man in a business age and society. He remodelled a castle for himself in the Isle of Wight and he built himself a princely town-house in Regent Street. There is some suspicion that he sold Mrs Nash to the Prince Regent for his patronage. He certainly lived in the Carlton House set, where manners were always superior to morals. At bottom he was a speculative builder with a genius for design. He died owing £40,000, and had himself buried at night to avoid arrest for debt. Yet nothing ever daunted him; he never shrank from the sweeping gesture or the grand opportunity. He was quite prepared, with the King's connivance, to sweep away Carlton House and convert old Buckingham House into Buckingham Palace, an enterprise which brought (rather unfairly) both financial and artistic discredit upon Mr 'Hash of Buck and Ham Palace'. In all this, and not only in the architectural field of town-planning, he may stand as a paradigm of Regency England. When all the pejorative adjectives have been expended—grandiose, superficial, slip-shod and the rest—he remains a giant in an age of giants and of the gigantesque, the age of Beethoven and Turner. And along with the gigantic, he shared in all the humanity, the charlatanry and the snobbery of the age which gave us Alfred Jingle and Mr Micawber. If everything that John Nash planned had been built, and if

Cumberland Terrace, Regent's Park, designed by John Nash, 1827

everything he built remained foursquare upon the earth, no
doubt we should be alienated by a gigantic pedantry, by the
incredibility of a dream come true, a dream ever in danger of
turning into a nightmare. As it is, we are charmed by fragments
and examples, gilded by time and distance. Sir John Summerson,
Nash's best biographer and exponent, has reminded us that
'the Regent's Park terraces are greatly loved today—more so
than they were when they were new. . . . The truth is that
these buildings, careless and clumsy though they are in many
ways, have an extravagant scenic character which, perceived
through nostalgic mists of time, makes them irresistible. . . .'
Nash himself, and the society in which, and for which, he
worked, is like that: a mixture of splendour and squalor, of
dream and reality, of such grandeur as consorts with Bath
stone and Parker's Roman cement, Coade Stone, and Hamelins's
mastic. If anyone insists that handsome is as handsome does,
Nash and his patron prince may justly reply: did any ever do
more handsomely than Cumberland Terrace?

Overleaf: *Regent Street, from the Quadrant*

Nash had a patron who spent money like water all his life. He never wanted for example in profusion. And here it is proper to record that in an age of laissez-faire, when the State is supposed to have withheld its hand from nearly everything that later times regard as its public duty, when 'central government did nothing to secure the public safety, provided no schools, gave no relief to the poor', it nevertheless was by far the greatest provider of funds for metropolitan improvements, and was thus the greatest, if indirect, employer of labour in the empire. Regency England is a little too readily portrayed in social history as 'The Age of Unrest', a heedless and heartless decade packed with Luddites, hunger-marchers and ragged Radicals. That is undoubtedly one side of the picture. The other side is to be seen in the Prince's London, its extravagant enterprises, its profusion, its restless gaiety, the brilliance of the over-dressed society which thronged its thoroughfares between the Regent's Park and St James's. It may be true that the people asked for bread and were given Bath stone. But the 'swinish multitude' were not altogether forgotten even at the height of the Regent's spending spree in 1814. One of Nash's tasks in designing the Peace Celebrations in the August of that victorious summer was the provision of suitable fun and games

'Five o'clock in Hyde Park'

Sir John Soane's masterpiece of the Greek Revival: the Bank of England

at the Fête of the People in the Green Park. He designed a Chinese Pagoda and Bridge. A good time was had by all, even though the Pagoda burst into flames and toppled into the canal.

The London of the Regency was not by any means exclusively the London of John Nash. To identify Regency Style with his classical façades would be to identify the part with the whole. To inscribe the name of John Nash above the whole picture would be to forget the magical contributions of Sir John Soane and the rising genius of Robert Smirke, both of whose names should not suffer eclipse by Nash's wholesale achievements. Soane is chiefly remembered for his pioneer work, at the Bank of England, for the Greek revival in the early nineteenth century. There is something eminently refined, even transcendent, about Soane's classicism, something scholarly and discriminating far beyond the bold and beautiful contrivings of John Nash. This is still to be experienced by a visit to the wonderful replica of his Art Gallery and Mausoleum at Dulwich. Soane's halls—notably at the Bank, the Court of Chancery, and Dulwich—with their lovely arches and lanterns, which seem to enshrine light rather than to encage it, achieving —in the words of Sir John Summerson—the Gothic miracle at the heart of the Roman tradition, these are something which add another dimension to the rectilinear splendours of the age. Smirke's name must stand with those of Nash and Soane in the Trinity of Regency architects, not only because he was one of

75

the three officially attached to the Board of Works, but by reason of his great memorial, the British Museum (1834-47), built for the housing of the Royal Library presented to the nation by George IV.

Nor should one allow the mind's eye to be monopolised by palaces and pleasure-domes, for a great deal of the improvement of London was concerned with the trading interests of the greatest commercial capital in the world. Our Regency visitor, Prince Pückler-Muskau, thought London much improved towards Regent Street, and was gratified by a personal visit to Mr Nash, but he passed by much of the architecture as 'monstrous' and turned his attention to what really interested him: Barclay's Brewery and the West India Docks. At Barclay's he recorded 12 or 15 barrels of beer brewed in a day, and everything done by machinery driven by a single steam-engine! At the docks and warehouses, he marvelled as men marvel at Rome or Venice. 'What a capital lies here in buildings, wares and vessels!' The West India dock, in the Isle of Dogs, was begun in 1800. The rest—the London Dock at Wapping, the Surrey, the East India, and (after an interval of twenty years) the St Katherine—all

Entrance to the Regent's Canal, Limehouse

The West India Import Dock, Poplar, with its impressive row of warehouses

followed in the 10 years before the Regency officially began. All were fine feats of planning, of engineering skill, and of 'tough refinement' in style. They began dockland as we know it today, in replacement of the old welter of mud basins, ramshackle wharfs and 'legal quays' downstream which had hampered rather than helped the traffic of London river for generations. At West India Dock the Prince admired the clear-cut grace of the great avenue of brick warehouses on their stone foundations. Goods to the value of 20 million sterling, 2,000 artisans at work with wonderful hoists and winches capable of unloading blocks of mahogany like feathers, and all closing down at 4 p.m. with the shutting of the great gates by the masterful gate-keeper, who said he wouldn't wait another minute, 'not even for the King'. This really was England, where trade was no respecter of persons, not even of princes. The English, the Prince reflected once more, certainly had a wonderful capacity for 'shutting up their property . . .'.

After Tyre, Babylon. After business, pleasure. The London of Hogarth, radiant enough by daylight where the parks gleamed in their greenery, but dark and stinking for the most part, was to stink for many a year yet, but light was coming to its

77

Lighting an oil lamp

opening vistas with the new coal-gas lamps. The Westminster Paving and Lighting Act had been passed in 1762, yet for another half-century London went by the feeble flicker of oil-lamps. Pall Mall was lighted by gas in 1807 by private enterprise, but the venturesome Gas Company had to suffer derision and opposition for many years from the vested interests of the whale-oil trade. The Bill of 1816, it was contended, would entail the ruin of the British Navy by destroying the whale-fisheries upon which it depended for recruitment, not to mention the ropemakers, sailmakers, mastmakers, etc., etc. Yet it was said by one historian of the time that 'the adventurers in gas-light did more for the prevention of crime than the Government had done since the days of Alfred the Great'. By lighting London effectively by night, they also enhanced the reputation of London as the City of Sin. 'London Lights' was to become a Victorian soubriquet for gilded immorality.

Night-life flourished in theatre, opera, circus, and in gaming-houses, billiard-rooms, clubs, pubs, and rooms. The flaring gaslight was appropriate to the hideous vulgarity of almost every form of public display and entertainment. It was yet a generation and more before the respectable citizen could take his family into London after dark for an evening's entertainment. Not until Henry Irving received a knighthood in late Victorian days could it be said that the acting profession received the accolade of respectability. The average bill of fare at Drury Lane or Covent Garden was what Prince Pückler-Muskau would have

Gas-works, near the Regent's Canal

called a 'mish-mash'. The usual programme at a London theatre consisted of a triple bill of a one-act play, a Shakespearian travesty, and a farce, salted with 'renderings' by a popular vocalist and possibly some conjuring-tricks. An operatic evening frequently 'executed' the opera by interlarding it with additional numbers or presenting an act from here and there—as if opera

A performance of 'Othello' at the Regency Theatre, Tottenham Court Road

were one big cake from which to cut chosen slices. Distinguished courtesans occupied front-line boxes at Covent Garden at perhaps £200 a season as shop-windows for their charms. At Astley's Circus and the Pantomime a night out was a roaring rough-and-tumble, a rough-house comparable to a session at the bear-pit or a cock-fight. At Crockford's, the Queen of the gaming-clubs, as much as £20,000 had been known to be lost and won in

The gaming-room of a fashionable London club

a single evening. Crockford himself had risen from making his living as a small fishmonger to presiding as 'the Scourge and Favourite of the Rich and Fashionable World'. Faro, Jeu d'enfer, blind-hookey, all were played in night-long sessions, and, although games of hazard were officially illegal in England, many Ministers of the Crown were members of Crockford's, and the Duke of Wellington was at one time a member of the managing committee. At the Argyle Rooms, membership was more exclusive than to have one's name in Debrett. The rooms were given over annually for the celebrated Ball of the 'Fashionable Impures', or 'Cyprians', where for one mad, glad night, 'the snowy orbs of nature undisguised', it was said,

The Cyprians' Ball at the Argyle Rooms: festival of the 'fashionable impures'

'heaved like the ocean with circling swell'. For the Boswellian reveller, the streets swarmed with common prostitutes. At the *Coal Hole* in Fountain Court off the Strand, the gay company of theatre-land kept it up till morning with chops and kidneys and rum-punch and song. At the *Brown Bear* or the *Cock* in the Haymarket or the *Craven's Head*, blind-hookey and strong liquor were to be had in company with John Thurtell and the flash-

The Vauxhall Gardens on a Gala Night

coves at any hour of the day or night. Vauxhall and Spring Gardens maintained their rather more salubrious modes of pleasure from the days of the ridotto and the masquerade.

The *ton*, or fashionable society, frequented a narrow quarter of London between Grosvenor Square and St James's, Bond Street and Park Lane, of which Mayfair was the centre. The City was left to the men of business and the law. The 'mobility' and the crooks frequented the rookeries east of Charing Cross.

Charleys

Indeed, whole neighbourhoods were populated solely by the vast underworld of a poverty-stricken and often half-criminal population. Considering the extent of poverty and crime within the bounds of the capital, the wonderful thing about Regency London is that the richest city in Europe subsisted for so long as an almost unguarded treasure-house. There was something more than a poetic truth in Wordsworth's description of the great city as 'lying open unto the fields and to the sky'. Of course, there were always soldiers in the barracks, despite prolonged opposition in the name of liberty to Pitt's policy of barrack-building during the war. There were the night-watchmen of the St Clement Dane's watch-house. There were the Charleys, descendants of Dogberry and Verges, with staves and lanterns, who sparsely patrolled certain respectable streets with their age-long if equivocal chant of 'twelve o'clock and all's well'. But not until Robert Peel's Metropolitan Police Act of 1829 had London the Force. Opinion was all (or almost all) against a regular, standing police force. It was suspect as a device of Continental tyrants. In the first year of the Regency,

A punch-up with the Charleys

the Wapping murders (celebrated so beautifully by De Quincey in his *Murder as a Fine Art*) put London in a panic. People seem to have preferred this, and the formation of private groups for security, to any organised peace-keeping force by public authority. 'I had rather half a dozen people's throats should be cut in Ratcliffe Highway every three or four years, than be subject to domiciliary visits, spies, and all the rest of Fouché's

The Press Yard, Newgate: a prisoner's chains are removed before execution

contrivances', as one gentleman wrote on that occasion. The Czar, Alexander I, visiting London at the Peace celebrations in 1814, took a curious interest in our laissez-faire attitude to public order and disorder. He thought it led to our having to punish detected offenders with great severity. A little preventive action as in Russia, he thought, would enable the authorities to let people off more lightly. Certainly the criminal code was extremely harsh. Scores of offences, some of which would now

A public execution

be classified as misdemeanours, carried the death penalty. So ferocious was the criminal code that a high proportion of condemned criminals were regularly respited, and juries frequently found verdicts of Not Guilty in the teeth of the evidence rather than consign the accused to the gallows for trivial offences. Men had yet to be persuaded—by jurists like Bentham and publicists like Romilly and statesmen like Peel —that terroristic punishment defeats its own purpose by increasing disrespect for the law as a 'hass'. The parliamentary Committee of inquiry into the Police of the Metropolis, 1816, revealed to the nation what every Londoner living east of the Park already knew, that the *Beggar's Opera* which purported to paint the underworld of London in the days of Walpole was if anything a pale shade of the London underworld of the Regency.

Further Reading

Thomas Burke, *London Night Life*
Denis Pilcher, *The Regency Style*
A Regency Visitor, Prince Pückler-Muskau (Ed. E. M. Butler)
Rowlandson and Pugin, *The Microcosm of London*
Sir John Summerson, *Georgian London*
— —, *John Nash*
— —, *Sir John Soane*

V

Politics

John Nash intended Regent Street to serve as a splendid avenue along which the nation's senators might drive to and from the imperial seat of government at Westminster. It was a preposterous piece of romanticism. British government was nothing like the government of imperial Rome. It had little to do with chariots and togas. Rather it was already a matter of cabs and drabs, gaslight and umbrellas. It had not even a great deal to do with London. Government came home to most Englishmen, in town and village, through squire and J.P., quarter sessions, parish beadles and overseers of the poor and the roving press-gang. At the head of the State, 'the collective wisdom' of the nation was dispensed by some six hundred M.P.s elected on a variety of franchises, or by none at all, and about half that number of peers who represented no one but themselves. The men who assembled in parliament, and produced the administration of the day, were at that time (as at most times) as mediocre a collection as could have been brought together by a random sample from the bran-tub of society at large.

The Prime Minister, Robert Jenkinson, second Earl of Liverpool, was known to his friends as 'Old Jenky' and to the cartoonists as 'the Blinking Son' of the first Earl, since he had a flickering eyelid. Disraeli christened him 'the Arch Mediocrity'. His administration was the pale shadow of that of Mr Pitt, whose principles and policies it imitated in all respects. 'Apish Jupiters', the Radical 'Black Dwarf' called them.

Robert Stewart, Viscount Castlereagh

There were men of distinction among them. Castlereagh, the masterly manager of foreign affairs, was of sufficient eminence (and unpopularity) to give the ministry his name in popular usage, viz. Shelley's hate-song, *Lines written during the Castlereagh Administration*. Wellington joined in 1818, as Master of the Ordnance, which lent the government distinction but aroused fears of military rule. When Castlereagh cut his throat in 1821, his old rival, George Canning, came in. Robert Peel succeeded Sidmouth at the Home Office in 1822. Indeed, the Liverpool ministry improved with age. It lived on, by blood transfusions, until its chief fell down in a fit in 1827. Its longevity otherwise was the result of three factors. In the first place, there was the absence of a viable alternative. The Whigs were divided, irresolute and ill-led. They were tepid, too often, about the war. When Spencer Perceval was assassinated in 1811, it has been said, almost anyone might have become Prime Minister. Liverpool came in as a stop-gap. 'I can assure you,' he told Wellington, 'I never sought the situation in which I find myself.' Secondly, Liverpool proved an excellent team manager, of exemplary patience and finesse. In the third place, the ministry (with the assistance of many thousands of soldiers and sailors, foundrymen, colliers, and cotton-spinners, not to mention farm-labourers) won the war. And when the war was over, and the social cleavages which it had concealed became dangerously apparent, enfranchised opinion was reluctant to change. Liverpool survived on the sentiment of 'safety first'. The government did little that was notable in the way of post-war reconstruction. It put its faith in what the Prime Minister called 'the gradual effect of the general policy of the government'. His policy seems to have been to have no policy. If he had been present at the creation of the world, a Frenchman observed, his advice would have been '*Conservons-nous le chaos*'.

86

Obviously, politics in these years were unlikely to be either heroic or inspiring. They were utterly unworthy of their environment in the London of the Regent and his architects. Nor did the grandiose building-schemes of the Prince and his town-planner extend to Old Palace Yard and St Stephen's. The Commons sat in a pit, or den, lighted by oil-lamps, and the Lords sat in a chamber 80 feet long, 40 feet wide and 30 feet high, tapestried, and with three semi-circular windows. Both were desperately over-crowded on any occasion of great debate. In 1834 both were burnt down as a result of the over-heating of the flues beneath the House of Lords; an affliction sent from heaven by an outraged deity, some said, after the passing of the Great Reform Bill. Barry's new buildings were begun in 1840. Thus modern Westminster possesses its neo-Gothic Houses of Parliament. What would Nash have made of such a commission 20 years earlier? He was never at his best in single free-standing public buildings, anyway.

The institutional life of politics and administration in the nineteenth century was subject to much satirical treatment by creative writers. Hardly any of the novelists, with the notable exception of Disraeli, could refrain from disrespect for those

A debate in the House of Lords

institutions which politicians and publicists so consistently praised as the glory of England. The cure for an unduly solemn attitude towards the House of Lords, it has been said, is to go and look at it. This has sometimes been recommended as an effective cure for an over-serious treatment of the House of Commons also. Samuel Bamford, the Lancashire weaver, visiting London in the winter of 1816, managed to obtain an order for admission to the gallery. He found himself looking down into a dim, lamp-lit den where were congregated 'some three or four hundreds of the most ordinary-looking men I had ever beheld at one view'. There were a few exceptions: Canning and Castlereagh, Brougham and Burdett. But 'what a scene was this to be enacted by "the collective wisdom of the nation".' They leaned against pillars with their hats cocked awry, they lolled on benches, stamped with their boots, snorted into neckcloths, whispered, coughed, whinnied, yelled, and howled like hounds at feeding-time. 'And are these, thought I, the beings whose laws we must obey? This "the most illustrious assembly of freemen in the world"? Perish freedom then, and her children too. . . . I turned from the spectacle with disgust, and sought my lodgings in a kind of stupor, almost believing that I had escaped from a monstrous dream.' Bamford's education was carried a step further when, in the following year, he was examined by the Privy Council, where he saw the oppressors of his country face to face. He harangued them, and they listened with patience and good-humour. Lord Sidmouth, the Home Secretary, watched him with mild, intelligent gaze; 'his manner was affable, and much more encouraging to freedom of speech than I had expected'. Lord Castlereagh turned out to be 'a good-looking person in a plum-coloured coat, with a gold ring on the small finger of his left hand on which he sometimes leaned his head as he eyed me over . . .'. These tyrants, he found, were even capable of a little mild laughter.

The gentlemen of the Privy Council confronting Samuel Bamford were looking upon a real live Radical, a member of a species generally described in parliamentary language as 'incendiary'. They knew little about each other, these polar opposites of the political scene. In an age which lacked the art of photography, those sections of society which rarely confronted each other in the flesh were veritably like ignorant armies that clash by night. Now, in 1816–17, they had met for one moment over a green-clothed table, had looked into each other's faces, had addressed each other in a common tongue. And all drama had gone out of the situation. The Radical had been bound over to keep the peace for 12 months. The gentlemen had been reproached for their proud indifference to the condition of the poor and distressed, and assured that 'the poor would be content could they only procure the common necessities of life by hard labour . . .'. The Ministers already knew this, but they were content to leave it to Providence and Adam Smith. As Lord Sidmouth was never tired of insisting: 'Man cannot create abundance where Providence had inflicted scarcity'. The Prime Minister agreed with him wholeheartedly, 'that in these cases the Legislature ought not to interfere, but should leave everything to find its own level'. Which, as Coleridge observed, is an ironical definition of a storm. Young Mr Weller paraphrased it succinctly: 'Every man for hisself, and God for all of us, as the elephant said when he danced among the chickens'.

Henry Addington, Viscount Sidmouth

The gentlemen concerned in this stately scene of governmental abdication were not proud and heartless noblemen of ancient lineage. Lord Liverpool was only the second of his noble line. So was Robert Stewart, Viscount Castlereagh, a courtesy 'Lord', but all his political life a most uncommon Commoner. Henry Addington, Viscount Sidmouth, was a son of a fashionable medical man who had dispensed port for the younger Pitt. The Lord Chancellor, John Scott, Lord Eldon, was a son of a Newcastle coal-merchant. He had worked his way to eminence from a grammar school by means of an exhibition to Oxford. Apart from the Lord Chancellor, they

89

John Scott, Lord Eldon

came from the gentry. In that sense they were natural governors. They were men who regarded politics as their particular and hereditary form of business, and they called tenure of public office 'employment'. Not that they were professional politicians in the modern sense. It was simply that they had been trained to regard it as their right and duty to rule England. They went into parliament as they went to public school and university, and as they joined White's or Brooks's or Boodle's. They were not rakes of the Regency. Political exigencies rather than personal tastes took them to Carlton House and the haunts of the Prince and the *beau monde*. They bore no resemblance to the dicing, duelling, dancing aristocracy of Old France. They were serious. They were men of business, attentive to the interests of a business nation. William Pitt was their idol, Adam Smith was their prophet, and, although on the whole they were lacking in imagination, they probably served their country, after their routine fashion, as well as any in that difficult and dangerous age.

For strange new forces were at work beneath the surface of politics. England was due to pass out of the age of humbug into the age of humdrum; from government by guesswork to government by statistics, from administration by unpaid amateurs to administration by professional and salaried servants. This transition was a necessity of a modern, largely populated, economically complex society. Lord Liverpool liked to believe that public peace and order could be maintained by the watchful influence of the squire—by those whom he called 'the gentlemen of the parish'. But everyone who had a responsible part in this work knew perfectly well that the country needed a professional police-force. Squire and parson still liked to believe that they could take care of the poor by neighbourly charity. But anyone who took a comprehensive view of the problem could see that the Elizabethan Poor Law, and the various patchings-up over the past two hundred years, would have to be replaced by a code based upon principles adequate to the vast changes that had taken place in the scope and nature of the problem. The Poor Law Amendment Act of 1834 was in the air for many years before it was enacted. When it came, it was based upon many of the ideas advocated by the Philosophic Radicals inspired by Jeremy Bentham, whose principles of rational legislation and administration were working everywhere in English society in the early years of the century. Benthamite Utilitarianism was steadily to become synonymous with enlightenment and progress.

Here is one of the great paradoxes of Regency England. Outwardly, it was an age of splendid building, extravagance and *brio* in dress and manners, dramatic—even melodramatic—achievement in arms and industry and engineering, the age of Turner and Constable and the Waverley novels, of Beau Brummell and Lord Byron and the Brunels. Inwardly, it was the age of an elderly and decidedly odd character who lived the life of a recluse at Queen's Square Place, Westminster, scribbling endless pages on law reform, parliamentary reform, the reform of the usury laws, the penal code, education, poor laws, in fact, reform of the world in general. Much of what Bentham wrote was unreadable. Nor was he ever an active politician. His mode of activity rather resembled that of Sidney and Beatrice Webb, the Fabian Socialists, a century later. He was the classic man behind the scenes—the man who taught the public men, principally the men of the opposition. And, as a prophet and teacher, he was that most dangerous of all teachers (dangerous in the sense of effective), the man of *un seul principe*. He had grasped (he was far from claiming to have discovered or originated) the single and immutable principle of human activity: that men seek pleasure and shun pain, and that the attainment of pleasure and avoidance of pain must be the sole principle, or touchstone, of all laws, institutions, and social arrangements whatever. Whose pleasure? Whose pain? That of the greatest number. Legislation could be reduced to a simple sum in arithmetic. Nothing else mattered, nothing else

91

Jeremy Bentham

can be taken account of. Political arithmetic is the whole art and science of government.

'The greatest happiness of the greatest number' might seem a commonplace objective for sentient beings. How could men seek less than this? How could they ever have needed to be taught to seek it? Bentham's work was to teach men, in detailed application, what the principle meant in practice. As William Hazlitt put it: 'Mr Bentham is not the first writer (by a great many) who has assumed the principle of UTILITY as the foundation of just laws, and of all moral and political reasoning: his merit is, that he has applied this principle more closely and literally . . . that he has . . . made a more constant and explicit reference to it at every step of his progress, than any other writer.' Hazlitt lived next door in Queen's Square Place, and he used to point out the great man as he perambulated his garden—a great philosopher who has made laws for all the world, but, as the sailors say, 'he has not allowed for the wind'. It was, and is, an easy criticism. But before Bentham taught his disciples, the test of English laws and institutions (if any) was anything and everything but utility in terms of the greatest happiness of the greatest number, any ancient prejudice, any selfish interest, any subjective criterion. The Philosophic Radicals who were taught by Bentham: Place, Romilly, Burdett, Brougham and the rest, came to serve as a leaven in the lump of English public life, working steadily and peaceably for a more just and rational order. Bentham's Utilitarianism was, like the master himself, 'the great questioner of things established', and stood (at its best) for the disinterested application of intelligence to social problems.

Jeremy Bentham died in 1832 at the age of eighty-five. The Philosophic Radicals were scarcely noticeable in the political scene until the 'twenties. The name 'Utilitarian' with a capital 'U' was invented in 1822. Neither the man nor the movement are readily associated with life in Regency England. But an age, like an iceberg, consists not only of the portion which shows above the surface. Politics under the Prince Regent might seem to consist only of the brightly illumined circles of Carlton House and Downing Street and Whitehall, of the Circumlocution Office, the Tape and Sealingwax Department, the haunts of Tadpole and Taper, of the Coodles and Noodles with their pocket-boroughs, and of a few ill-assorted Radicals kicking-up a shindy at Spa Fields or St Peter's Fields in Manchester. In fact, a great deal of cerebration was going on at Queen's Square Place, and down at Ford Abbey in Devon, where Bentham rented a summer residence for some years from 1817 onwards; and at 16 Charing Cross, where Francis Place, the master breeches-maker, had by 1820 made his premises into 'the headquarters of English Radicalism' or a 'Civic Palace', alias 'the gossip-shop' of reformist politics. At Rodney Terrace, Pentonville, Bentham's most ardent and influential

'The Peterloo massacre': the rally at St Peter's Fields, Manchester, 16th August 1819

Francis Place

disciple, James Mill, was composing his essay on *Government* which, when produced as a sixpenny reformist tract in 1820, seemed to establish an unanswerable argument for the reform of the House of Commons on Utilitarian lines, and did more than any other single act of propaganda to capture the junior intelligence of England (and especially among the youth of Cambridge) for the cause.

The Benthamite, or Philosophic, brand of Radicalism was chiefly influential with the young of the middle classes. It was too intellectual, too high and dry, to make much appeal to the generality of the working classes at that time. But Radicalism of a direct, knife-and-fork variety, as preached by men like William Cobbett and Major John Cartwright and dozens of pot-house politicans among the working men themselves, was thriving in the industrial districts. 'The Politics of Bread' was the offspring of suffering. It was nourished by the hope which seemed to have dawned for the betterment of the lot of common humanity with the French Revolution. The artisan and the day-labourer had entered into political life in the 1790s with such organs as the London Corresponding Society, the first organs of a truly political character ever established by the people and for the people. The possibility of the people taking the initiative and engaging in a genuinely popular politics was startling and abhorrent to the traditionally political classes of society. As one satirist put it:

> *Shall those who drudge from morn till night*
> *Pretend to talk of wrong and right?*
> *No, no, the sweat which toil produces,*
> *Exhausts the intellectual juices.*

Nevertheless, this was what was happening, now. It was in Regency England that the name 'Radical' was coined, though its precise meaning was never established. Sir Walter Scott said it meant any fellow in a ragged jacket. Little Charles Dickens, who was born in 1812, thought it simply meant a species of 'terrible banditti' which were to be prayed against.

William Cobbett relieving the industrious labourer

Radical principles, he understood, were 'that the Prince Regent wore stays; that nobody had any right to any salary; and that the army and navy ought to be put down . . .'.

That good Victorian lady, Harriet Martineau, looking back from the mid-century, found it difficult to credit the alarm caused in her girlhood by the Radicals of the Regency. It was astonishing, now, 'to think how great was the panic which could exist without any evidence at all: how prodigious were the radical forces which were always heard of, but never seen . . . how country gentlemen, well-armed, scoured the fields and lanes, and met on heaths to fight the enemy who never came:

how, even in the midst of towns, young ladies carried heavy planks and ironing-boards, to barricade windows in preparation for sieges from thousands of rebels whose footfall was long listened for throughout the darkness of the night.'

Miss Austen, who did some of her best work in those years, could not believe that such alarm was justified by anything but the horrors of the circulating libraries. No rational creature, in her opinion, could have been referring to anything else when talking of 'horrors expected in London . . . a mob of three thousand men assembling in St George's Fields; the Bank attacked, the Tower threatened, the streets of London flowing with blood'.

But then, Miss Austen had never a high opinion of human credulity.

The literary ladies were scornful of the 'alarm': Miss Martineau, thinking of the alarm caused by the machine-breakers at the very opening of the Regency years, was being wise after the event; while Miss Austen, writing at the time of the Spa Fields riots in the winter of 1816, was wise before the event, for the Cato Street Plot was not discovered until 1820.

The threat of the Radicals: Sir Francis Burdett at the Middlesex election

The men who blacked their faces, and took sledge-hammers to the stocking-frames, were not revolutionaries but local saboteurs driven to desperation in defence of their livelihood. They had few coherent political notions, and showed no sign of planning a general confederacy of labour. Working-class politics had little if anything to do with pikes and muskets and sledge-hammers. They had everything to do with peaceful petitioning for parliamentary reform. Their activities took place not in cellars and garrets but rather in public-houses and disused chapels, in the Hampden Clubs founded by political 'field preachers' of reform like the venerable Major John Cartwright, or in Corresponding Society branches which had survived from the 'nineties. As Samuel Bamford is never tired of assuring us in his *Passages in the Life of a Radical*, the village politicians stood firm by the advice given them by the Major: 'Stand fast by the laws.' On the whole, they aped their betters, the liberal gentlemen who were so often their patrons and were proud of being 'constitutionalists'. Despite many disappointments, they generally preferred to go along with Sir Francis Burdett and the Major, rather than to look for a working-class Robespierre or Marat.

Yet they found one for a few hours on a June night in 1817. Jeremiah Brandreth, 'The Nottingham Captain', came among the stone-cutters and foundrymen and peasants of the Notts and Derby border with a mission to lead a rebel army to Nottingham, where they would join forces with contingents from all over the Midlands and the North, a vast concourse bound for London, where Sir Francis Burdett, Major Cartwright and other radical gentlemen were awaiting them with a Provisional Government (Brandreth's men seem to have thought that a provisional government had something to do with provisions). Brandreth had probably been a Luddite. He behaved in a bloody, bold and resolute manner on the march to Nottingham, and he talked the language that had been held in the neighbourhood by a spy, the notorious Oliver, though there is no evidence that the two men ever met. He recruited his army partly from the more hot-headed Radicals of the border villages, and partly by the forced enlistment of farm-servants who were

Jeremiah Brandreth

routed out of their beds en route at the point of a gun. One, tardy in joining the ranks, was shot. It was this reluctant element in the rebel contingent that melted away in the early morning light as the army entered Nottinghamshire. Some miles from Nottingham a small company of dragoons appeared in sight, and the ranks broke and fled. Brandreth himself vanished until he was taken in bed in Sheffield a few hours later. A few months later, three principals in this tragi-comedy were executed at Derby, and many more shipped off to Botany Bay. Many of those indicted for high treason wore smock-frocks in the dock. There was no one involved who could possibly have been described as a gentleman. Brandreth himself was in receipt of parish relief. In fact, the Derbyshire Rising (still known locally as 'The Pentrich Revolution') is the solitary example in Regency England of a radical movement made entirely of, by, and for working men. Unless it was made by Oliver the Spy—an over-simple answer favoured by Radicals of the parliamentary opposition, the Press and the history-books ever since.

Preference for leadership by men of quality was not simply the snobbish heritage of a class-ridden society. It was a shrewd instinct that told them that (in Disraeli's phrase) 'in England even treason, to be successful, must be patrician', or at least that the gentlemen knew how to lead, if they would. They also had a habit of living to fight another day, and if you proposed to change the House of Commons, there was much to be said for having at your head some one who sat there. As tribunes of the plebs, Major Cartwright and Sir Francis Burdett might be cautious, but they were not cowards. They also, or so it appeared, were men of impeccable sexual morality: an important consideration with working-class politicians at all times, and especially at this time when popular politics went so closely hand-in-hand with nonconformist religion. Cobbett, as prudish as any Victorian, was finally alienated from Orator Hunt when he heard that Hunt went to mob-meetings in a barouche accompanied by another man's wife. At the height of his popular influence Cobbett took to wearing a swan's-down waistcoat and generally dressed the part of a gentleman farmer. Henry Hunt always made the most of his pretentions to be a country gentleman, and lost nothing in the eyes of the great crowds who turned up at his oratorical performances by his elegant coat and his doeskin breeches, his topped boots and his white top-hat. His dress gave to his tall and well-proportioned figure the authentic mould of a Corinthian or a Regency buck. It is significant that the greatest demagogue of his age sought to assume the image of the fox-hunting squire, and few things are more pathetic than the account given by Bamford in his memoirs of his disillusionment about Hunt's character after Peterloo.

There was undoubtedly a raffish, melodramatic streak about radical politics in that raffish, melodramatic age. To snatch up sword or dagger and strike a blow for freedom and the dispatch of tyrants was an appropriate gesture in an hour when the style of ancient Rome was all the rage in rhetoric and architecture. Arthur Thistlewood, at his trial for the Cato Street Conspiracy, spoke from the dock after what he supposed was the style of Brutus. Was he encouraged in his fantasy by the very name of 'Cato Street'? Besides, panic-mongers like Burke had taught men to believe that revolution came with a single, mighty, bloody blow, and it might be true. . . . And yet, the true genius of the time, in the sense of authenticity in terms of achievement, may better be discovered in the pedestrian style of the Benthamites quietly engaged in their mole-like workings. Here, at the political level, we come once more upon the paradox of life in the Regency. Within a stone's throw of Queen's Square Place where the elderly philosopher was showing his disciples the road to the future, Arthur Thistlewood, seedy ex-officer of militia, is showing a handful of thugs in a stable-loft in Cato Street the way to assassinate the Cabinet by girding themselves with swords and pistols, not forgetting certain bags and carving knives for removing

Henry Hunt

99

The Cato Street Conspiracy, 23rd February 1820: the plotters surprised

and carrying away heads, later destined to be borne along on pikes to the meeting of the Committee of Public Safety in session at the Mansion House. They would rush into the dining-room of Lord Harrowby in Grosvenor Square with the cry of: 'We have better men here than your Manchester Yeomanry!' But the Cato Street Conspiracy was to be frustrated before the *émeute* could commence, and the principals hanged at Tyburn.

By that time, the Prince Regent was King George IV. But the atrocious fantasy of Cato Street is every bit as representative of one element in his reign as the peaceful labours of Jeremy Bentham are of another. George Borrow, whose books afford us so many glimpses of that violent, vivid, spasmodic England that Bentham and Thomas Gradgrind never knew, was prepared to supply a swan-song for the Cato Street tradition. 'Oh, there was something in those fellows!' And all because Thistlewood had vindicated the old tradition by running a sword through a police officer. He probably thought no less highly of Jeremiah Brandreth who had shot a reluctant recruit while putting on his boots.

Further Reading

Samuel Bamford, *Passages in the Life of a Radical*
E. Halevy, *History of the English People in the Nineteenth Century*, Vol. I
James Mill, *On Government*
M. W. Patterson, *Life and Times of Sir Francis Burdett*
Donald Read, *Peterloo: the Massacre and its Background*
Graham Wallas, *Francis Place*
R. J. White, *Waterloo to Peterloo*

William Cobbett, M.P.

VI

Manners and Morals

'He has the manners of a Marquis and the morals of a Methodist', it was said of one of the bad baronets of Ruddigore, those typically stylish scoundrels of the Regency.

It was intended to express a rare and startling conjunction, rarer and more startling at that time than at any other, with the possible exception of the Restoration. For the Regency has borne an ill reputation in the history of morals. Popular fiction from Thackeray to Jeffry Farnol has invested the term with an aura of rakish manners and polished vice. And the raffish air

A dandy at his dressing-table

which strikes posterity as so typical of London society at that time is no myth invented by novelists and journalists of a later age. The cartoons of Gillray, or the memoirs of a man-about-town like Captain Gronow, or a lady of the *ton* like Harriette Wilson, all yield the authentic aroma. 'How unspeakably odious . . .', the Captain wrote, looking back in the eighteen-sixties to the Age of the Dandies. No doubt he was thinking of characters like the limping Corinthian, Lord Barrymore, better known as Cripplegate, and his brothers Hellgate and Newgate, and their foul-mouthed sister, Billingsgate. When Harriette Wilson wrote her memoirs in retirement, she was to express no regrets for an ill-spent life. Her purpose was, quite frankly, blackmail. Harriette was nothing if not frank. So was the Duke of Wellington. 'Publish and be damned', was the Duke's response to Harriette's ultimatum. None the less, buying one's self out of Harriette's memoirs became a full-time occupation of the peerage in the later 'twenties.

Like the Restoration, the Regency was a period of moral (or immoral) reaction. During the active reign of the old King, the Court had experienced a prematurely Victorian régime of propriety. In fact, it had been a very dull place. The King and Queen, with their numerous progeny, had set a standard of decorum and domestic virtue which did much to drive the royal sons, as they grew up, into the company of profligate persons of both sexes, an errancy which in its turn did much to drive their well-meaning but mistaken father out of his wits. This had now been accomplished. At almost the same time that the old king went into a strait-waistcoat the ladies left off their stays, while the Prince of Wales took to wearing corsets. Petticoats also were shed, and women began to wear knickers just at the time when the men were ex-changing breeches for 'trowsers'. Strait-lacing went out; and high busts and loosely flowing gowns came in. Vast feathered hats and high-piled coiffures gave place to bonnets and fringes, or bunches of corkscrew ringlets. At the opposite extremities, bootees and sandals reflected the fashionable classical mode. Eurhythmic dances like the minuet gave way to the darting flurry of the waltz. This last was thought to denote a general decline in moral standards, if not the onset of national decadence. Lord Byron affected to think that the waltz encouraged wantonness; but then, he was always something of an Evan-gelical manqué, and his malformed foot made waltzing difficult. The middle classes, notorious

A lady of fashion

103

The waltz

for morality in all ages, were disposed to frown upon modern manners and morals as typically wicked perversities of aristocracy, and perhaps they were right. Much of the loose-living of Regency England arose from the perennial and old-established laxity of an aristocracy which had never ceased to do what it liked and cared only for its own whims. After all, aristocracy shines by its own light and owes nothing to popular (which generally means middle-class) opinion. As Miss Pamela Fitzgerald wrote to a friend in 1816, 'the vices were wonderfully prolific among Whigs', and most of the great families of the age were Whig families. The Tory country gentlemen tended to stay at home in their country houses while the great Whig lords rioted in Babylon. They were always a free-spoken promiscuous lot. Their daughters, as one matron said fondly, were 'comfortable girls who like a dirty joke'. Among them were to be found the Harleys, children of the Countess of Oxford, known as the Harleian Miscellany because they all had different putative fathers. High and low linked hands in this, as in so much else. 'There are such countless illegitimates,' Miss Fitzgerald continued her letter, 'such a tribe of children of the mist.' Alexis de Toqueville, visiting in 1833, commented upon the low state of morals among the country people. 'Many country women become pregnant before marriage. The number of bastards is increasing. . . .' But then, to become a farmer's wife, a young woman had to prove her fertility.

Certain lines were drawn, however. Unnatural vice was frowned upon, especially by the Prince Regent, who liked his vices simple, clean and straightforward. Sodomy was still a capital offence. A London jury took only ten minutes to find a verdict against a waiter accused by a stable-boy in 1815, and the man was executed promptly, although large numbers of thieves and murderers were respited, as usual. 'Some people drink to forget their unhappiness', wrote the unhappy William

Beckford in 1812, 'I build.' He wished he could live in London, but the social ban on him kept him behind the high walls of Fonthill. Silence reigned over the flight of the Marquess Townshend in 1812. Homosexuality was known to be wide-spread at that time, but the law was strictly enforced, and the conspiracy of silence was preserved. One bridle upon behaviour was Beau Brummell's creation of the beau ideal of the gentleman *de nos jours,* and his princely patron's insistence upon his own role as 'The First Gentleman of Europe'. Edmund Burke had protested in a famous passage on the ancien régime in France, that vice lost half its evil by losing all its grossness. Even if this were true, it would scarcely acquit the Regency of its guilt. Loose-living under George, Prince of Wales, either as Regent or as King George IV, was often as coarse and dull as it had been under George I and George II. The Prince himself set an example of gross feeding, drinking and whoring which, at first sight, assorts strangely with his tastes in the finer arts.

But the Prince was an anachronism. He was playing Charles II, without the wit, refinement or political skill, more than a century too late. The world, and especially the English world, was passing out of the era of profligate princes into the century

Domestic life of the aristocracy

The Regent (right) and his uncle

of citizen-kings, umbrella-bearing presidents of crowned republics. He knew this, in a general way. 'In these unhappy times, Sir,' he once wrote to his father, 'the world examines the conduct of princes with a jealous, a scrutinizing, a malignant eye.' But he never did anything much about it. All around him, noble lords had their coats off, improving the breed of pedigree cattle, building canals, governing state and empire. The Prince, having outlived or parted from the friends of his gilded youth, never grew into the political maturity of a man who was to wear a crown. Falstaff departed, and the Prince came to his regency as a stout and waddling man of very nearly 50. He was happiest showing his guests round the Pavilion, which he did with the utmost charm and the most condescendingly uncondescending manner, or putting his foot down on the subject of flat roofs which let in the rain. He felt, he wrote to John Nash, that the use of mastic on roofs, was 'most inconsiderate conduct . . .'. In town, he presided over the building of a classic capital for an empire whose achievements rivalled those of Caesar and exceeded those of Napoleon, or so it was claimed, achievements for which the Prince felt himself to be personally responsible. When, at long last, British arms met with victory in Spain, he begged his mother 'do not quite forget poor me, who have I think some little merit at having been the first to set them all to work', and when Napoleon was overthrown in 1814, he thought 'perhaps I may be vain enough to hope that you may feel a little proud of your son'. As he grew older he grew ever more firmly convinced that he had fought at Waterloo, a fantasy which may have originated in a desire to annoy the Duke of Wellington.

It is all too easy to recall only the ageing roué, the 'Prinny' of

Mr Creevey's letters and diaries; the fearful old rip coming up to London from Newmarket or Brighton in the dark so that no one should see his legs or discover whether he could walk; the maudlin monarch weeping between Lady Conyngham and the Princess de Lieven on a sofa in a crowded drawing-room. This elderly, corseted Adonis was still the father of Regent Street and Cumberland Terrace, the man who loved the novels of Jane Austen and who made Walter Scott a baronet. The friend

Royal Pavilion, Brighton: the Steyne front, by John Nash, 1815–20

of Scott, the patron of Nash, the recipient of the Dedication of *Emma*, could perhaps dispense with the moral approbation of Thackeray. He ate too much and drank too much and he spent money like water. He lacked every middle-class virtue except a real fondness for his ugly mother and sisters. But his vices were plain profligacy, not a refined form of satanism. There were many men of more blameworthy moral life in the higher ranks of his realm. He bears the most opprobrium because he bore the highest rank of all. It would be ridiculous to accuse

Regency à la mode

him of corrupting the Regency, though there is something to be said for the notion that the Regency corrupted him. He was, said the Duke of Wellington, 'the most extraordinary compound of talent, wit, buffoonery, obstinacy and good feeling—in short a medley of the most opposite qualities, with a great preponderance of the good, that I ever saw in any character in my life'. And the Duke saw a great many.

The line between the Respectable and the Low, which was to be drawn so clearly in the Victorian years, was already pretty plain. But it was not yet the poverty-line. The situation was confused by the tendency of the upper classes of Regency England—and especially their young—to ape the manners of their inferiors, to adopt the manners, the dress, the demeanour and the pastimes of *hoi polloi* as a fashion. At intervals, throughout the last two centuries or more, the young have indulged in such periodical bouts of *nostalgie de la boue*. The Mohock, the Blood, the Teddy Boy, the Moll, the Angry; tight trousers, crew-cuts, gamin hair-styles, the cult of dirty skin: all have been symptomatic of this passion for disguise under some aspect of disreputability, disgust or desperation. In Regency times the fashion adopted by young gentlemen of quality took the form of dressing like a coachman or a bruiser. Young gentlemen 'sported democrat', or Jacobin, or some other species of (so it was thought) desperado. You wore a whole series of capes, like a coachman, and a conical beaver like a tall toadstool, and you carried a whip. You tipped the professional driver of the mail to let you take the 'ribbons', or you drove your own 'bit of blood' to a phaeton, or curricle, or gig, down the road to Brighton or Bath or wherever, at breakneck speed. You adopted the language of the expert in horse-flesh, and practised swearing and spitting tobacco-juice with the rapidity and range of a bargee. To crop your hair and swagger about in vast swathes of neck-cloth, a sash, or skin-tight boots and pantaloons, after the guise of a pugilist, was particularly popular. You liked to be known as a Corinthian, a buck, or a bang-up blade. The best and oldest of these affectations, that of the bruiser, was often based on a real proficiency in the science of fisticuffs on the part of the man of family. Two generations of the squires of Felbrigg, in North Norfolk, bore the nickname of 'Boxing' or 'Fighting' Windham between 1717 and 1810 (the younger serving as Secretary at War under Pitt); both were men of taste and some scholarship.

It was a special characteristic of the Regency, this adoption of the pastimes of the mobility by the nobility, or by the upper classes in general. When pursued by people with virtually unlimited money and leisure, such pastimes held much temptation to corruption. A mill, or a knock-down fight with bare fists, became a sporting event which engaged the attention of half England. 'I have known the time', Lavengro records,

A sparring match at the Fives Court, St Martin's Street, London

A prize fight

'when a pugilistic encounter between two noted champions was almost considered in the light of a national affair; when tens of thousands of individuals, high and low, meditated and brooded upon it, the first thing in the morning and the last thing at night, until the great event was decided.' Such an encounter was likewise the occasion of frenzied laying of bets; likewise the rigging or crossing that are liable to ensue when large sums of money are at stake. Hazlitt tells us in his fine essay, *The Fight* (1822), how the nobility and the mobility of half England assembled for the famous fight between Bill Neate and the Gas-man at Hungerford, when £200,000 was at stake. Thomas Burke in his *Murder at Elstree* (1936) has given us a vivid account, from the career of John Thurtell, of the skulduggery and crime that could follow upon 'crossing' or tampering with the course of a match in which many have much to win or lose.

'Pity that corruption should have crept in amongst them', sighed George Borrow, looking back to the halcyon days of the great pugilists. For the bruisers of England had been the high priests of the old religion of England—the religion of the Ring —and Lavengro strings their names like a rosary: Cribb and Belcher, savage Shelton and the terrible Randall, Ned Turner and Bulldog Hudson, the fearless Scroggins and Black Richmond,

and Broughton and Slack and Ben. . . . Another celebrant might
have said the same of cricket at that time, chanting the names of
the giants of old: Lumpy Stevens and David Harris, Illustrious
Sackville, the Nyrens and the Hambledon men. The 'laws' had
been established since 1774. The three-stump wicket, the four-
and-a-half-inch bat, the six-seamed ball, the M.C.C., Lord's
ground—all were established by the opening of the Regency.
But cricket, like boxing, was suffering corruption by the
money-power, and was going through a dark age. And here
again, the trouble was the 'legs', the backers or promoters
who managed the match, which too often meant that they
bought and sold it. Finance was the weakness of cricket in the
days before the County Clubs with their professionals in receipt
of regular wages, talent money, and benefit-matches. Before
this, only the gentlemen could really afford to play a game which
took up so much wage-earning time, and the burden of financing
a side generally fell on their shoulders. The poorer players
were eminently, and understandably, bribable. 'Just in front
of the pavilion at Lord's, at every great match,' we learn, 'sat
men ready, with money down, to give and take the current
odds upon the play.' Even the famous Crockford was not unknown to attend. And the Marylebone legs were not content
with straight-forward betting business, but were prepared to

A sport for gentlemen: cricket in 1821

buy up the leading professionals to turn the game the way they
wanted it.

This corrupt state of affairs was at its worst in the years of
the Regency. Moreover, the Regency found cricket in the
midst of one of its periodic crises about throwing. Round-arm
bowling, or over-arm as we know it, was regarded as throwing
when it was first practised at speed, and only made its way to
orthodoxy in the late 'twenties, and into the 'laws' of the game
in 1835. Its exponents called it 'the new liberal system'. Its
opponents were prone to barrack, to invade the pitch, to pull
up the stumps and bring the game to a standstill, thus doing
something that even the Luddites never achieved in the ways of
intervention. In June 1817, when an England Eleven was to

Professionalism in cricket: the England v. Sussex match, played at Da

play Twenty-two of Nottingham at Nottingham, notorious at
that time as a centre of machine-breaking and later as the
stamping ground of Harold Larwood and body-line, the magis-
trates warned the players that they could not be responsible
for the consequences unless stumps were drawn by seven in the
evening. It transpired that the crowd which swarmed on to the
ground at that hour simply wanted to see the eleven who had
contended with twenty-two. This match has been said to mark
the close of prehistoric cricket. Certainly the middle age of the
game dawned with the round-arm revolution of 1828. By the
mid-Victorian years, cricket had undergone the middle-class
revolution which we associate with the Great Reform Bill and
the decline of corruption. It had still, however, to be reconciled

Sheffield, in 1827, as a trial for the new round-arm bowling

A box at the opera

with organised Christianity. As early as 1744 it had been charged with unseemliness in bringing gentlemen, clergy and lawyers together with butchers and cobblers, with withdrawing large numbers of people from their employments, and with openly encouraging gambling. A hundred years later, it was still a rather disreputable pursuit, on account of the gambling element. The great Mr Felix, who kept a private school for the sons of gentlemen, adopted that name as a pseudonym, for the good name of the school; rather as John Brodribb at about the same time decided to take the name 'Henry Irving' in order to spare the family name from association with the stage.

Everything was for sale: pocket-boroughs and prize-fights, curacies and cricket-matches, and the professional ladies of the *ton*, whose display-cases were the boxes at the opera and the carriage-drive in the park. The Fashionable Impures they were felicitously called, or—more simply—the Cyprians. Variously and individually they bore such names as The Venus Mendicant, The Mocking Bird, The White Doe, or Brazen Bellona. The greatest of them was Harriette Wilson, the veritable Queen of Tarts, otherwise referred to as Harry, or The Little Fellow, not because there was anything diminutive about her, but from sheer affection. Not that Harriette resembled that cynically sentimental novelist's creation,

Ladies of fashion in Hyde Park

the great-hearted whore. She was as hard as nails. She was rather matey than romantic; frank and familiar, or comfortable. She was not even staggeringly beautiful. Her attraction seems to have lain in her alluring figure, her fine colouring, and her abounding vitality. Daughter of a Swiss watchmaker and a stocking-mender, one of many children, and several fair daughters, Harriette took up with the Earl of Craven (the

Le beau monde

opening sentences of her *Memoirs* typically record the fact without reference to causes or motives), was established in a succession of elegant apartments, and never looked back—or down. The noble lords came, and were entertained, and were more than willing to pay. Entertained in the widest sense, for Harriette educated herself by experience of educated companionship. She must have provided a bracing change from domestic dullness and formality. Her clients did their social duty to their families, begat the necessary heirs, and duly put in an appearance

Harriette Wilson

beside their spouses on all suitable occasions. They went to Harriette for life, ease, and wit. It would be ridiculous to say that she provided the tripe and cow-heel suppers after the decorous dinners at home, but there was a flavour of *nostalgie de la boue* about her crowded evenings, with the stairs thronged from top to bottom with noble company, and life belowstairs lapping over into the drawing-room. Harriette, too, was an excellent mimic and an expert in the cut-and-thrust of fashionable badinage. She had the spirit of the age in her gusto and mischief. Her high spirits, rude vigour, and frank enjoyment, lent a quality unique among the great courtesans of history. The life of that small, profligate and extremely expensive world which centred upon Mayfair and the Steyne bore little resemblance to either the brittle brilliance of *la vie parisienne* or the lush romanticism of Sunset Boulevard. Even the bawdy of the Regency, while it lasted, was fun. Harriette Wilson's *Memoirs* must always rank as a serious, if disreputable, historical document.

Further Reading

H. S. Altham, *A History of Cricket*
Correspondence of William Beckford (Translated by Boyd Alexander)
Leslie Branch, *The Game of Hearts* (Memoirs of Harriette Wilson)
Thomas Burke, *Murder at Elstree*
Roger Fulford, *King George the Fourth*
Captain Gronow, *Reminiscences*

VII

Scenes from Provincial Life

The best of England was always provincial England, and the happiest people lived their uneventful lives in small country houses. There is a great difference between a country house and a house in the country. Country houses belong there and are a part of their environment. A house in the country is 'a rural retreat', built to be visited at certain times in the year for change and refreshment. In Georgian England, many houses were built in the rural scene for this purpose. They had all the sophistication of town houses set down in the country, their urban faces looking out upon gravel and lawn which came up to the footings. The Regency still built 'displaced town houses' of this type, but the notion had spread abroad that, while the neat stuccoed box with pillared portico and fanlights was very well at Marylebone or Hampstead and perhaps in the main thorough-fare of a county town, the edge of the village or deep country made a better milieu for pointed windows, perforated iron-work verandas, virginia creeper, and a roof-line pricked into crockets and pinnacles. When Cobbett declaimed against Mr Montague's little place down in Hampshire, with its attempt to look like a church with crosses made of bits of Scots fir nailed together, it was Cobbett the countryman rather than Cobbett the aesthete who spoke. He disliked Mr Montague's taste because of Mr Montague's origins: he was an intruder from the City. But the Gothic taste was already flourishing, and was showing itself a favourite for rural solitudes. The Grecian style remained the accepted style for large public buildings, with compulsory portico and columns, at least until Barry created the new Houses of Parliament in pointed style in 1840. Robert Smirke's British Museum and General Post Office are famous examples, in their 'chaste inanity', and at Cambridge William Wilkins imported the style into a University town full of Tudor red-brick when he began to build Downing College in 1807. But, all the time, the taste for neo-Gothic was growing rapidly, fulfilling the passionate search for the picturesque which chiefly cherished the irregular, the asymmetrical and the surprising. It amounted to an aesthetic war of Goths versus Grecians, and those who took part in it knew very well what they were doing, for in the early years of the century expert architectural writers were producing text-books for their guidance. Payne Knight's *Analytical Enquiry into the Principles of Taste* came out in 1805, and Thomas Rickman's *Attempt to Discriminate the Styles of English Architecture* in 1819, provided the technical names that were to last, 'Early English', etc. Ecclesiastical Gothic was generally bad. It had a way of looking what it was: mock. But most people seem not to have minded this, so long as it was picturesque. James Wyatt made his fortune out of the perversities of pastiche.

The Gothic, fanciful and bastardised as it often was, seemed to consort best with rurality. With its irregularities, its hump-backed roofs, its spikiness, its generally sombre air—or its amusing fantasticality, however one cared to view it—it fell in conveniently with pointed pines, sprawling oaks, pendant ivy and creeper. It was snug. People who sought rural peace and quiet congratulated themselves on escaping from the stilted and stately mansion to the homeliness of low ceilings and the intimacy of hole-and-corner rooms. Even the Regent had tired of his seaside palace at Brighton and was happiest in the little snuggery of York Cottage. The *cottage ornée* was often a town villa draped with creeper, ringed with ironwork veranda-posts and roofing, weighed down and darkened by heavy overhanging thatch. The more it looked like a keeper's cottage or a lodge at the gates of a great house, the more willingly one put up with smoking chimneys or dripping eaves. So important was it that the place should radiate rurality, that one gentleman provided for a fire to be kept going in perpetuity, long after the cottage ceased to be inhabited, simply in order to ensure a suitably rural aspect from afar. For what was a cottage chimney without smoke? Smoke had been the principal embarrassment of people who built in the Palladian style, with its pure roof-lines, almost innocent of protruding chimney stacks—as permitted by the

Cottage ornée: Endsleigh Cottage, Milton Abbot, Devonshire

climate of the Mediterranean lands. . . . As for snugness, it was well-known that the lords of such palaces as Chatsworth lived in the kitchen, or some poky corner of the house for warmth and ease, and had not Dr Johnson said of Lord Scarsdale's great house at Kedleston: 'It would do excellently for a town hall'? Of course, those who could afford it might have both the Grecian palace and the *cottage ornée* in Gothic

119

A neo-Gothic country house: Luscombe, near Dawlish, Devonshire, designed by John Na.

detail. There were cases where people tried to have both in one. Where husband and wife divided between Classical and Gothic, they might have the front of their house in one style and the back in the other. There never was a single Regency style. The amount of pastiche and divergence from norms that studded the land is a sure sign that one could hardly call it an age of taste.

The neo-Gothic itself, where it appeared, was often of the Strawberry Hill variety: Gothic as seen by eyes that retained the Classical lines upon the retina. The little church of Saint Mary the Virgin and All Saints at Debden in Essex shows charmingly, on its west side, what the notion of Gothic was to its builder round about the year 1800, while the east chapel, with its ribbed plaster vault is plainly a Strawberry Hill version of the Chapter House at York Minster. Finally, the Gothic was cheap. By 1825, almost all Gothic mouldings or ornament could be bought wholesale. From the *Gentleman's Magazine* in 1818, we learn that 'there is scarcely an ornament or a necessary part but what might be cast at one Iron Foundry; even the highest wrought filigree Gothic'. In this sense, appropriately perhaps, the Gothic revival may be said to have been a child of the Industrial Revolution. In 1827 there appeared Robinson's *Designs of Ornamental Villas*, and in 1830 *Village Architecture*. The democratization of Gothic was certainly at hand. 'Carpenter's Gothic' or 'pure Batty Langley' the artists called it. What it could produce for sheer charm may be seen in the new Rickman building at St John's College, Cambridge, especially when the creeper is out.

The people who lived in the country houses, large and small, as distinct from the houses in the country, Georgian or Gothic, —parsons, doctors, lawyers, half-pay captains, rentiers—the professional class in general, made themselves comfortable behind their pleasant façades, old and new, with little concern over architectural styles, managing to live some of the quietest and most placid lives on record. Indeed, so quiet that record is rare. Historical record of these lives is mainly to be discovered in the novels of the time, and is most faithfully preserved in the works of Jane Austen. From the genius of this 'chiel amang ye takin' notes', this assiduous polisher of her own small pieces of

Young ladies at home

Boys at play

ivory, posterity is privileged to see the serenely busy lives of this small society like an ant-hill in sunshine. A wider panorama, though in less depth of penetration, may be seen in Mary Russell Mitford's *Our Village* (*c.* 1825). At a slightly lower social level, William Howitt's *Boy's Country Book* (1839) painted freshly, in simple colours, his memories of rural life in Derbyshire. Jane Austen gives us the gentlefolk, mainly within doors, their small dramas, their hearts and heads, contrivings, and fortunes. Miss Mitford, because she takes the village rather than the family for her subject-matter, gives us a vivid impression of the populousness of country life: 'men, women, children, cows, horses, waggons, carts, pigs, dogs, geese and chickens, a busy, merry, stirring little world'. Provincial life was busy enough to those who lived it, although to a later age it may seem unbearably uneventful and tame. The boys, like most boys in most ages until subtopia engulfed them, had their country pastimes, bird-nesting, pony-riding,

Adults in miniature

rough shooting over stubble and pasture, their fire-side games and hobbies. The girls had their samplers, their music, and a host of household tasks in preparation for the time when they would have households of their own. All was training for the great adventure of being grown-up. In fact, both sexes were treated like men and women in miniature rather than as a special species known as 'youth' with special claims upon the rest of the world for its service. They grew up later than the children of Tudor or Stuart England, but still a good deal earlier than the children of the twentieth century. On the

122

whole they do not appear to have been unduly bored or resentful.

Early schooling was generally conducted at home. The Victorian women who grew out of this time frequently possessed a toughness of mind, an intellectual power, which they undoubtedly owed to their having received their girlhood instruction from fathers or elder brothers, more especially where the male elders were of the clergy or a learned profession, rather than from governesses and boarding schools. Private schools were mostly inferior even to the old local

An academy for young ladies

grammar school with its Latin grind. Miss Pinkerton's academy for young ladies, on Chiswick Mall, was an expensive establishment devoted to turning out the young lady 'not unworthy to occupy a fitting position in [her parents'] polished and refined circle'. Provincial young women—and young men, if they were not sent to one of the great schools—received a more utilitarian type of instruction with less exalted ends in view. The girls practised a great deal of needlework, music and dancing; both sexes practised ornamental penmanship, a sporadic memorising of where foreign parts lay and what they produced, and a

Girls at play

routine knowledge, highly spiced with moral judgment, of the kings and queens of England. Goldsmith's *History of England*, in which haloes and halters are handed out with the unfaltering certainty of the Day of Judgment, was the favourite text-book. Here, Alfred was good, and John was bad for 'he showed his contempt for religion by habitually swearing'. Henry VIII was 'cruel from a depraved disposition'. And so on, down the list, to George III, 'our gracious and beloved sovereign, whom God preserve'. The Rev. Mr L. M. Stretch, master of the Twickenham Academy, wove morality into his historical fabric with even greater pertinacity, in his *Beauties of History*, or pictures of vice and virtue drawn from real life, designed for the instruction and entertainment of youth, in two volumes. Here we find history teaching from the examples of Cleopatra, Cardinal Wolsey and John Hampden. As Miss Austen makes Mr Tilney say: 'I often think it odd that it should be so dull, for a great deal of it must be invention. . . .' However, Mr Henry concluded: 'That little boys and girls should be tormented is what no one at all acquainted with human nature in a civilised state can deny. . . .' These offspring of provincial parents in modest but comfortable circumstances left school literate, with a smattering of the classics, a fraction of French, able to write an elegant hand but not to spell too well, and to solve simple sums in arithmetic. Above all, they left school grounded in 'sound principles of religion and morality'.

A young lady

The domestic interior of such lives varied from elegance to homely comfort. Probably the average décor is to be seen in the 'best parlour' of Robert Southey's Somerset kinsmen among the well-to-do clothiers: a well-proportioned room with a black boarded floor covered with a Lisbon mat, the pictures curtained to keep off the flies, a handsome timepiece over the fire-place, a tortoiseshell cabinet filled with china, a

Children's games

fire-screen of embroidered silk, a kidney-shaped writing-table, cherrywood armchairs, and mezzotints in black Brazilian frames. Of course, to have a best parlour was regarded as slightly vulgar, a somewhat tradesmanish notion, by the lesser gentry. To them, tables and chairs by Sheraton, or in the elegantly brittle tradition of that master, and heavier furniture whenever possible rested on feet carved into the likeness of the claws and paws of the greater birds and beasts. Pedestal tables, cerule chairs, gilded beasts as supporters, bits of Egyptian ornament and bric-à-brac, these elegancies consorted well with muslin-swathe gowns and high waists and knee-breeches for evening parties. They lent the correct classical tone to a society which prized elegance without disdaining ease. The thing that delighted the foreign visitor about the English domestic interior more than anything else, after all, was the armchair. Prince Pückler-Muskau did not spend much of his time in provincial households, but everywhere he went he detected the prevailing English genius for making themselves comfortable in a sitting posture.

The English at home had not yet rejected card-games as the invention of the devil. They played whist for half-crowns, and *vingt-et-un*. They drank spruce beer and mead, mostly home-brewed. Port and brandy were by no means regarded as solely medicinal. The social part of the day really began at, or after, dinner, which was by this time growing later than it had

'The English domestic interior'

A card party

formerly been: between three and five. Tea might be drunk at
six or half-past, but in town it was generally later. In provincial
households servants were cheap and plentiful, but the sons and
daughters of the house were at this time tending to do more for
themselves. The young women washed the best china and clear-
starched their own linen; the young men took an active part in
looking after the horses. They took their part *with* the
domestics, who were intimate members of the household. One
old woman and a stableman might be the sum-total of staff in a
provincial establishment: familiars rather than retainers. The
daughters of Samuel Botham, a surveyor and land-agent of
Uttoxeter, mingled refined tastes in literature with domesticity,
to the extent of reading and declaiming poetry over the starch-
bowl. This was how they rejoiced over Moore's *Lalla Rookh*
when they managed to borrow a copy. 'It was the day when we
clear-starched our caps; we declaimed the poetry while we
clapped the muslin—read and clapped alternately.' Like most
young women, they kept albums in which they copied out their
favourite verses in the finest copper-plate.

Diversions, among these country families, consisted mainly of

127

Balls at the Assembly Rooms in the County town and of visiting neighbours. Not the formal 'visiting' of leaving cards, but short sojourns in each other's houses at a distance, involving all the excitement of cross-country journeys in a post-chaise over deep mirey roads and through snow and ice. More infrequently they made visits to Cheltenham, or Matlock, or some inland spa; even to Bath. Cheltenham Spa, Papworth's elegant achievement with its tree-lined Parade, its tall Classical houses replete with the latest elegancies in iron-work and balconies, was the typical inland spa of the Regency. Leamington Spa had developed famously since 1808: the population of the new town increased from 315 to 6,000 between 1801 and 1820. The Regent himself stayed at what became The Regent Hotel in 1819. Such excursions, with their adventures in the way of coach and carriage spills or an occasional fall on the Cob at Lyme Regis, provided some of the red letter days of a quiet provincial life-time.

And there was the seaside. The English were at this time coming into their national heritage. They ruled the waves with their navies and their merchant fleets. They were, even if the best of them had 'inland far their setting', the sea-faring people *par excellence*, and an annual visit to the waves they professed to

The Montpellier Pump Room, Cheltenham, designed by J. B. Papworth, 1827

rule had a certain tonic effect on the emotions as well as the physique. In fact, in the later eighteenth and early nineteenth century, the English citizen was fast becoming sea-conscious, and the seaside-holiday industry was beginning to boom with all its paraphernalia of 'lodgings to let', bathing-machines, marine parades and special catering for visitors. In 1819, Miss Austen made it the subject of *Sanditon*, her last and unfinished novel. Here we meet Mr Parker, the complete enthusiast for Sanditon. 'The success of Sanditon as a small, fashionable Bathing Place

Bathing-machines in Bridlington Bay, Yorkshire

was the object for which he seemed to live. . . . A few years ago, and it had been a quiet Village of no pretensions: but some natural advantages in its position, and some accidental circumstances having suggested . . . the probability of its becoming a profitable speculation, they had engaged in it, and planned and built, and praised and puffed, and raised it to a something of young renown—and Mr Parker could now think of very little besides. . . . He held it indeed as certain that no person could be really well . . . without spending at least six weeks by the sea every year. The Sea air and Sea Bathing together were

nearly infallible, one or the other of them being a match for every Disorder of the Stomach, the Lungs or the Blood . . . We have all the Grandeur of the Storm, with less real danger, because the Wind meeting with nothing to oppose or confine it around our House, simply rages and passes on. . . .' Mr Parker's Sanditon consisted of only a few cottages, but 'the Spirit of the day had been caught, as Mr P. observed with delight . . . and two or three of them were smartened up with a white Curtain and "Lodgings to let". . . .'.

The therapeutic virtues of Sanditon (according to Mr P.: 'Anti-spasmodic, anti-pulmonary, anti-septic, anti-bilious and anti-rheumatic') were the most important part of the advertisement. Those who hoped commercially to exploit the sea, made a point of insisting upon the health-giving properties of sea-water as a beverage. Dr Richard Russell's *Dissertation on the Use of Sea-water* had been published as early as 1752, and was by no means the first to prescribe it as a specific for almost all the ills that flesh is heir to. As for sea-bathing, Floyer and Baynard's *History of Cold Bathing* had been enjoining it since

130

...pular seaside resort

the beginning of the century. The revolting practices of drinking sea-water, and immersing the body in it, were probably the more acceptable to the middle classes because they involved pain as well as pleasure, and could therefore be enjoyed with a good conscience. Visits to the seaside, like resort to spirituous liquors, could be labelled 'for medicinal purposes'. After all, seaside towns were called 'resorts'.

There was nothing particularly new about this recourse to the waters. As Horace Walpole once said: 'One would think that the English were ducks; they are for ever waddling to the waters.' But then, he was talking about the fashionable practice of the eighteenth century in visiting Bath, or Harrogate, or Tunbridge Wells. The eighteenth century was the great age of the inland watering-place, or the 'Spaw' as they called it. It had been going on for a very long time, and those who took part in this kind of exodus were aristocrats or persons of the upper middle class who could not only afford it but could, and did, appear unabashed in the company of their betters who set the prevailing tone. The bells were set ringing when Lord Tom

Noddy drove into Bath, a happy practice that was later to accompany the arrival of wealthy bourgeois citizens at Brighton and elsewhere. But the seaside watering-place, with the possible exception of Scarborough ('The Queen of the Northern Watering-Places') which as a seaside spa had been frequented since the early years of the seventeenth century, was in general less exclusive. Here the shop-keeping middle class of the age of the Prince Regent was beginning to appear *en famille,* though the real exodus to the coast only became multitudinous after the coming of the railways. The south end of the village of Prittlewell was already emerging as Southend-on-Sea, complete with Royal Terrace since the sojourn of the Princess Charlotte and Caroline, Princess of Wales; by 1794 it already had 'the romantic library, the elegant card-assembly, and coffee-rooms'. Brighthelmstone was already beginning to look like Brighton, principally by reason of the patronage of the Regent himself who spent much time there after 1783. The south-west, all along the coast from Kent to Cornwall, was ripe for development

The Steyne, Brighton. The Chain Pier, erected in 1822

after the old King took to staying at Weymouth for con-
valescence after his several bouts of mental disorder. His
earliest visit was a royal progress westward in 1789, and as
long as he could travel he went to Weymouth. The extended
range of royal approval consequent upon a visit to Christchurch
Bay was to work wonders in the almost virgin regions of
Mudeford and Bournemouth. Where royalty went, and what
royalty did, the great middle class could go and do likewise,
after its fashion.

What did they do at the seaside in Regency times? They
sniffed the ozone and were 'dipped' (by stalwart characters
called 'dippers', of whom the most famous were Martha Gunn
and Old Smoaker at Brighton); they went for walks or carriage-
drives and picnicked at picturesque or historic scenes; they
danced at the Assembly Rooms, and frequented the circulating
library. The library purveyed a great deal more than books,
Minerva Novels and periodicals. It was something in the nature
of a superior 'drug-store' after the American style. The ladies

ain Brown, R.N., stood until 1896 when it finally collapsed

Seaside relaxation: Hall's Library at Margate

could spend hours there, gossiping, sampling, purchasing. The
Public Rooms where you could take tea or coffee while the
band played were mostly descended from the Rooms at Bath
and the inland spas. They had a good deal to do with the
preservation and improvement of manners, with their rules of
dress and deportment, generally based on the famous decrees of
Beau Nash at the Bath Pump Room. Margate, which by its
proximity to London, had quickly become extremely popular,
and was already in the 1780s coming under fire as 'devoted to
gaiety and dissipation', had rules for the Assembly Rooms
obviously framed upon the Beau Nash model. Dancing to begin
at 8 o'clock and to end at midnight precisely; no ladies admitted
in habits; no gentleman in sword, boots or pantaloons (except
genuine military gentlemen). . . . As long as travel was slow
and expensive, exclusiveness was maintained by distance. For
coach-costs were often prohibitive even to the moderately well-
to-do. As Mr Knightly retorted, in Miss Austen's *Emma* (1816)
to Mr Woodhouse's eulogy of Cromer, he would be most
willing to prefer Cromer to Southend if someone could tell

him how to convey a wife and five children a distance of 130 miles with no greater expense or inconvenience than a distance of forty. . . .

It was the railway that founded the modern fortunes even of Southend and Margate, although Margate was served by the famous Margate hoys—single-masted sloops of some hundred tons burden—which carried thousands of holiday-makers down

The morning promenade at Cheltenham

from London even before one of the Brunels brought the first steam-packet to Margate in 1814. The tripper-traffic had arrived before the railway. 'You think Margate more lively', Cowper once wrote. 'So is a cheshire-cheese full of mites more lively than a sound one. . . .' What, now, was to become of the sublimity of the ocean which had been one of the fashionable concepts of the age of sensibility? Jane Austen had mocked at the sublime language of Sir Edward Denham in *Sanditon*: 'He began in a tone of great Taste and Feeling, to talk of the Sea and the Seashore, and ran with energy through all the usual phrases employed in praise of their Sublimity, and descriptive of the *undescribable* Emotions they excite in the Mind of Sensibility. . . .' Sensibility had scarcely yet ceased to claim its martyrs. Mrs Sarah Fletcher, who died at Dorchester in Oxfordshire in 1799, at the age of 29, was said in her epitaph

The arrival of the Margate hoy

to have died 'a Martyr to Excessive Sensibility'. *Sense and Sensibility* was published in the first year of the Regency, 1811.

Further Reading

W. Addison, *English Spas*
Jane Austen, Novels
Martin S. Briggs, *Goths and Vandals*
Sir Kenneth Clark, *The Gothic Revival*
John Gloag, *English Furniture*

William Howitt, *The Boy's Country Book*
Christopher Hussey, *The Picturesque*
Bryan Little, *Cheltenham*
R. Manning-Sanders, *The English Seaside*
Mary Mitford, *Our Village*
J. B. Papworth, *Rural Residences*

VIII

The Puritan Revival

Morals, like most things in England at that time, tended to go by classes. Top and bottom of society had much in common. The middle had its own standards, and already laid great store by respectability. As James Mill put it, the middle rank was 'the class which is universally described as both the most wise and the most virtuous part of the community'. Mill, who belonged to that rank, also held that 'the opinions of that class of the people who are below the middle rank, are formed, and their minds are directed by that intelligent and virtuous rank, who come the most immediately in contact with them . . .'. It was particularly important, at that time, that the lower classes should be set a standing example of moral restraint in sexual behaviour. Otherwise, as the Rev. Thomas Malthus was believed to have shown conclusively in his very depressing *Essay on the Principle of Population* (1798, 2nd ed. 1803), numbers would outstrip subsistence and there would be an inevitable decline in living-standards all round. An aristocrat like Shelley denounced the 'hardened insolence' of any proposal to rob the poor of 'the single alleviation of their sufferings and their scorns . . . the soothing, elevating and harmonious gentleness of the sexual intercourse and the humanising charities of domestic life', while Cobbett advised the 'monster' Malthus to go and preach moral restraint to Brisk Tom and Smart Sally at the church-door. But the middle classes scarcely needed Malthus to teach them the virtues of continence. Evangelical religion was strong among them, and consorted well with their worldly interests. They understood well enough that the virtues of a Christian after the Evangelical model were easily exchangeable with the virtues of a successful merchant or a rising manufacturer.

The Evangelical revival—unlikely as it may seem—reached its height in the years of the Regency. The native moralism of the English had re-asserted itself, and, as might have been expected, it assumed the outward form of a reformation in manners. It was long overdue. A revival of propriety was in part a defence against the vulgarity which had been creeping into society with the arrival of

A Wesleyan Chapel, Liverpool

what the old King had once called 'mere moneyed men'. Too much wealth too quickly (and often dubiously) acquired; too many jockeys, bruisers, clowns and whore-masters accepted by the Prince and his entourage; a lowering of tone, and a superficial emphasis on *ton*; the raffish cultivation of the art of living on nothing a year—as exemplified by fringe characters like Rawdon Crawley and the adventuress, Miss Sharp: all these things, and many more, had corrupted the Georgian standards of manners. The murder of Mr William Weare in 1822 by John Thurtell at Elstree provided the typical *cause célèbre* of the time, with all its stylish brutality.

> *They cut his throat from ear to ear,*
> *His brains they battered in.*
> *His name was Mr William Weare,*
> *He lived at Lincoln's Inn.*

John Thurtell was a 'flash cove' who had arrived—for a moment —at national eminence after a brief career among the Gentlemen of the Fancy, who revelled at Covent Garden and the Haymarket. At his trial a witness offered testimony to his respectability with the famous observation: 'He was a respectable man. He kept a gig.' Whereupon, Thomas Carlyle promptly coined the Synonym for Respectability: Gigmanity. It was, as Carlyle would have said, 'a sign of the times'.

And behind the recourse to respectability was the memory of the terrible fate which had overtaken a godless and immoral society at the time of the French Revolution. It reinforced the more distant memory of the Divine chastisement of the Portugese (who were immoral enough to allow themselves to be ruled by the Jesuits) by the Lisbon earthquake of 1755, when several thousand persons had been killed in a few minutes. London had experienced several quite noticeable quakes in 1750, and Manchester had suffered one in 1777, occasioning the observation of John Wesley: 'There is no divine visitation which is likely to have so general an influence upon sinners as an earthquake.' When the French Revolution set off carnage and slaughter across the Channel, the reaction of the propertied classes in England was exemplary. The poor were astonished to see so many carriages at the church-doors of a Sunday, and domestic servants began to find themselves paraded to morning-prayers in the drawing-room. The revival of the practice of family prayers was widely noted in early nineteenth-century England.

A crowded church service: the interior of St Andrew's, Plymouth

By this time, moral rearmament was beginning to appear
almost as a necessity for national
self-preservation. It seemed to
be an aspect of the nation's
defence against genocide. Drink,
disease, 'soul-murder' and 'self-
slaughter' (especially of factory-
children), all seemed to cry
aloud for the reformation of

Dr Simeon, the great evangelical preacher

morals, for the cultivation of personal and social responsibility.
After sojourning for long in the cold formalism which so often
served eighteenth-century men and women as a substitute for
faith, the English were linking themselves up with their
seventeenth-century traditions of pietism and the Puritan conscience. Not that there had ever been a complete break, for the
intervening century had been the age not only of Parson
Trulliber but of Parson Adams, not only of Hoadley but of
Law and his *Serious Call to a Devout and Holy Life*, not only of
the Hell Fire Club and John Wilkes, but of the hell-fire sermons
of Whitefield and John Wesley. Resumption of a providential
outlook was hastened by experience of calamity in the form of
the American and French revolutions, or the prospect of their
fell repercussions upon England. Young poets felt constrained
to proclaim the need for national repentance.

> *We have offended.   Oh my countrymen!*
> *We have offended very grievously.* . . .
>   *Therefore evil days*
> *Are coming on us, O my countrymen!* . . .

Thus the young Coleridge in 1798 as he scanned the waters
from Quantock for the coming of the French invasion-fleet,
bearers of 'the flail of God'.

Like everything else in that aristocratic society, moral reformation began at the top. Selina, Countess of Huntingdon, the
Duke of Grafton, that reformed rake at Euston, were among the
first to set an example (according to their own peculiar

notions) of holy living and holy dying. Nor must the example of His Majesty, King George III, be forgotten. 'The good old King' (the older and madder he got, the more his virtue was celebrated by his loving subjects) had set an example from the first days of his reign as a very self-conscious exponent of high moral principles in both public and private life. One of his earliest actions had been the issue of a proclamation against vice and immorality. In the year 1787, William Wilberforce persuaded the King to continue the good work with another proclamation, this time followed by a Society, or Vigilance Committee, to watch over the actual *suppression* of vice (among persons with less than £500 a year, the Rev. Sydney Smith said). This was in 1802. That year saw the publication of Thomas Bowdler's *Family Shakespeare*. The purified version of the Bard went into six editions in one year of the Regency (1818). Bowdler replaced the word 'body' with the word 'person' throughout, 'in the interests of Decency and delicacy'. Within another 10 years the same treatment had been extended to *Robinson Crusoe* by the Rev. James Plumptre of Clare College in Cambridge. The famous fourteenth and fifteenth chapters were left out of Gibbon's *Decline and Fall of the Roman Empire*, Mr Bowdler gleefully announcing that Shakespeare and Gibbon could 'no longer raise a blush on the cheek of modest innocence nor plant a pang in the heart of the devoutest Christian'. The Victorian Age was born long before the accession of Queen Victoria. Mr Podsnap's repudiation of everything calculated to call a blush into the cheek of the young person, was in force half a century before Dickens published *Our Mutual Friend* (1865).

An improving book

It would be absurd to attribute this kind of silliness to reaction to 'the excesses of the French Revolution'. Tom Moore thought that the Revolution had the tendency 'to produce in the higher classes of England an increased reserve of manner, and, of course, a proportionate restraint upon all within the circle, which have been fatal to conviviality and humour, and not very propitious to wit . . .'. But the cult of reticence and of respectability was more than a prudential fashion in an age of revolution. Nor is it at all simply to be ascribed to premature Victorianism, unless Victorianism is the proper name for a mood which settled down all over northern Europe in these years, far beyond Mr Podsnap's island specially blessed by Providence 'to the Direct Exclusion of such Other Countries as there may happen to be'. It was part of the *gemütlichkeit*, the cult of a smug domesticity, enjoyed by the prosperous middle classes everywhere in these lands. Even there, of course, a conscientious satanism was maintained in some quarters: a persistent element of romanticism, especially among the poets. Byron, Beckford, Beddoes, Bailey (of *Festus* fame)—all the Bs before Browning—retained a rake-hell style on occasion. If you were a good enough (or perhaps bad enough) poet, even the pious were ready to wink the other eye. Those virtuous poetasters, William and Mary Howitt, laid their hands reverently upon Byron's coffin when it rested at the *Blackamoor's Head* in Nottingham, and William trudged in the noon-day heat the six miles out to the vault at Hucknall Church to see the end of the hero. In such minds, Byron's libertinism was outmatched by his liberalism.

On the whole, reaction against the French Revolution may be said to have driven virtue into alliance with the Tories. Virtue captured the Premiership with Spencer Perceval on the eve of the Regency. He was assassinated by a lunatic in the lobby of the House of Commons shortly afterwards. However, his successor, Lord Liverpool, was to devote much time and energy to promoting the Church Building Act of 1818, by which the state allocated a million pounds for the erection of new strongholds against dissent, infidelity and democracy in London. Two hundred and fourteen churches were built, 174 of them in the Gothic style, mostly in brick, many with cast-iron columns supporting the galleries. The Commissioners in charge of expenditure and contracting were dominated by the need to house the largest possible congregations at the lowest possible cost. They recommended a type of portable font which could be had at fourteen shillings, and sacramental plate in Britannia Metal at £3 19*s*. a set. 'The improprieties and absurdities comitted in the mass of paltry churches', said A. W. N. Pugin, 'is a disgrace to the age.' But Lord Liverpool had identified the Regent's government with the cause of virtue and of truth.

A prophet who explicitly disavowed the identification, or even the alliance, of Christianity with the cause of improvement, was liable to desertion and repudiation by patrons and disciples alike. Robert Owen, the master manufacturer of New Lanark, published his *New View of Society* in 1813. It was dedicated to the principle that 'any general character, from the best to the worst, from the most ignorant to the most enlightened, may be given to any community, even to the world at large, by the application of proper means; which means are to a great extent at the command and under the control of those who have influence in the affairs of men'. He taught a more or less total environmentalism, and he practised it. He was prepared to save the world, and cure all its ills, by parallelograms, or villages of co-operation, at a very moderate sum per head. His model factories and villages at New Lanark were visited by kings and noblemen from all over Europe, and the Tory cabinet were deeply impressed. The man seemed to have found the cure for the problems of the Poor Law. But when, in 1817, Owen thought good to announce to a public meeting that the principal enemy of human betterment was religion, the noblemen, cabinet ministers and bishops withdrew in a hurry. It was plain that the man was

The Gothic revival: National Scotch Church, London, by Sir William Tite

unsound on Original Sin. This should have been plain to anyone from the very beginning. So Robert Owen went on alone—so far as the powers that be were concerned, or unconcerned.

Robert Owen

The Evangelical movement, headed by the Clapham Sect, might be described at the time of the Regency as the praying section of the new Tory party of Pitt. Intensely humanitarian and ardently philanthropic, its leaders—cultivated and genteel persons like William Wilberforce and Hannah More—worked passionately for the redemption of souls at home and for the abolition of black slavery and the infamous slave-traffic abroad. *Practical Christianity* (1797), Wilberforce's testament to the inspiration and aims of the Evangelical movement, went through fifteen editions down to 1826. But the Evangelical idea of salvation was not salvation by books, or theology, or intellectual argument. 'God has set before me as my object the reformation of my country's manners', wrote Wilberforce, early in his career. That was what 'Practical Christianity' meant: the promotion of personal salvation by right conduct. 'I know that by regulating external conduct we do not change the hearts of men', Wilberforce confessed; 'but even they are wrought upon by these means. . . .' It was the heart that mattered. The hearts of men were to be 'got at'. Indeed, there was a good deal of the cult of feeling—so typical of the Romantic movement in poetry—about the movement. Weeping for joy was a speciality with Wilberforce. He caused Arthur Young, the great agriculturist, to go blind in his later days by making him join him in tears over the death of the Duke of Grafton, despite a warning that the old man's emotions must not be disturbed. In 1820, on returning from an unsympathetic interview with Queen Caroline as a member of a Commons' deputation, he burst into tears over a humble moss rose in the garden. 'Oh the beauty of it, oh the goodness of God in giving us such alleviations in this hard world. . . . And how unlike the Queen's countenance.'

THE
SHEPHERD
OF
SALISBURY-PLAIN.

Title-page of an early tract

The Evangelicals put enormous faith in tracts. The Religious Tract Society was founded in 1807, and thence proceeded a deluge of these cheap editions of moralistic fables. *The Shepherd of Salisbury Plain* (1809) was the prototype of the species. Hannah More, the most cultivated lady convert of the Clapham Sect, was the best-seller, and from her flowing pen proceeded not only tracts for the humble but books for the well-disposed middle and upper orders. *Thoughts on the Manners of the Great* (1809), and *Practical Piety* (1811), not to mention the immensely successful anti-novel, *Coelebs in Search of a Wife* (which contained a manifesto against drama, poetry, and romance as vehicles of 'unparalleled vice and infidelity'), contributed much to the divorce of piety and intellect and did more than anything to produce the hopeless imbecility of so much Evangelical writing and preaching. 'They are perpetually calling upon their votaries for religious thoughts and conversation in everything', complained the Rev. Sydney Smith. 'No Christian is safe who is not dull.' By 1818 we find Tom Moore warning Leigh Hunt to keep off religious and moral subjects. 'The mania on these subjects being so universal and congenital that he who thinks of curing it is as mad as his patients.'

William Wilberforce

When he came back to England from self-exile in America in 1819, William Cobbett was chiefly struck by the deterioration in public taste which was denoted by the fashion for tracts. 'Never did we, until these days, hear of millions of Tracts, Moral and Religious. . . .' Parson's sermon, once a week, used to be sufficient religion for the village.

146

'Now we had a busy creature or two in every village dancing about with "Tracts". . . .' This fashion was nothing but canting hypocrisy. 'There were indeed thousands, if not millions of examples of this species of homily hawked about the country. . . .' The mission of the 'Saints', he held, was simply 'to teach people to starve without making a noise . . . keeping the poor from cutting the throats of the rich.' Hence their continual harping on spare diet, living simply and frugally, and being thankful to one's betters. Like the Methodists, they pursued a crafty policy of postponement: preaching the virtue of concentrating the mind on the Heavenly Crown, turning the minds of poor men to

William Cobbett

the Heavenly Mansions when they needed decent cottages. Cobbett tells us of the country girls listening to a fellow preaching like this at Benenden in Kent. They seemed 'to be thinking much more about getting houses in this world first: houses with pig-styes and little snug gardens attached to them, together with all other domestic and conjugal circumstances. The truth is,' he concludes, 'these fellows had no power over the minds of any but the miserable.'

If Cobbett made a dead-set at the Saints of Clapham, it is well to remember that they made a dead-set at him. For he was an immensely influential writer, and he always believed (and said) that the best religion was one that made men innocent and benevolent and happy 'by taking the best possible means of furnishing them with plenty to eat and drink and wear'. Hannah More, and her sister Martha, at their evangelistic mission among the Mendip miners, were teaching them to read—to read the Scriptures, not Cobbett's Political Register, or 'The tupenny Trash', and were proud to report that their pupils were sending up professions of loyalty to King and Constitution. 'All we allow, by way of a song, is "God save the King". . . .'

In an age and a society so robust and racy as Regency England it is to be expected that tractarian religiosity should meet with repulsion and satire. For one thing it was an age of fine, strong, masculine prose-writing: the age of Cobbett, Hazlitt, Jeffrey and the *Edinburgh* reviewers. True, the best-remembered satire came a little later, with Thackeray's Lady Emily Sheepshanks, author of *The Washerwoman of Finchley Common* and *The Sailor's True Binnacle*, and Wilkie Collins with Drusilla Clack in *The Moonstone*. Miss Clack's encounter with the discontented cabman is typical: 'I paid the cabman exactly his fare. He received it with an oath; upon which I instantly gave him a tract. . . . He jumped up on his box, and with profane exclamations of dismay, drove off furiously . . . I sowed the good seed, in spite of him, by throwing a second tract in at the window of the cab.' But satire was easy. The tracts presented a target impossible to miss. And before Victorian satire reached its best, the literature of the Evangelicals was dead. No literature ever died to such swift and utter oblivion. The tracts of Clapham are remembered now only by their Victorian parodies. The millions of grubby little pages of newsprint that poured from the Religious Tract Society are as well-trodden out of remembrance as the fallen leaves of a Regency autumn beneath the trees of the Regent's Park, aside from a few pressed specimen's in a collector's cabinet or on the shelves of the British Museum, anticipating the fate of the comic-strips, and much science fiction of today. Hannah More and Sarah Trimmer and Mrs Sherwood lived to see the day when 'Tractarian' meant Oxford and John Henry Newman. Nor should it be forgotten that a genus has its species. After 1827 we have Lord Brougham and the Tupenny Trash of the Society for the Diffusion of Useful Knowledge, and Miss Martineau's threepenny tracts, *Illustrations of Political Economy*. Evidently there are tracts—and Tracts.

Evangelicalism, for all its trivia, was one of the great formative forces of the nineteenth century. It generated much of the moral energy which transformed the England of the Regency, with its robust, and often coarse, immoralism, into the England of Victoria, serious, philanthropic, morally responsible. It is a far cry from the Regent's Park to Clapham Common, as far as from Babylon to Jerusalem. Along with the parallel and often allied movement, Utilitarianism, Evangelicalism served to justify, and even redeem, the wealth and power of the middle classes with a creed. It was a creed which taught and practised personal responsibility, the discipline of unsleeping watchfulness in the conduct of daily life, the duty and happiness of philanthropy. It has been said that while Utilitarianism,

A Sunday school

with its cult of universal rationality, provided cant for practical men, Evangelicalism with its zeal for holiness, provided cant for serious men, and that both mistook respectability for grace and identified corruption with the low. By their works shall ye know them. Both were at war with cruelty, vice and brutality. Between them they ended the slave trade and inaugurated the New Poor Law. Evangelicalism was vital religion. It was moral rearmament. It was practical christianity. It conquered.

Further Reading

N. G. Annan, *Leslie Stephen* (Chapter 3)

Amy Cruse, *The Englishman and his Books in the early 19th century*

E. M. Forster, *Marianne Thornton*

F. J. Harvey Darton, *Life and Times of Mrs Sherwood*

M. G. Jones, *Hannah More*

Sir Harold Nicolson, *Good Behaviour*

R. K. Webb, *Harriet Martineau*

IX

The Dawn of the Age of Seriousness

When peace came to Europe in 1815, the English discovered the Continent once more. For twenty years, with scarcely a break, they had been shut up in their island, cut off from the refreshment of Continental experience and ideas. When peace came, they flocked abroad to see what they had been missing. 'Everything was new and fresh', writes Haydon, who was among the first to visit Paris. 'We had thought of France from youth as forbidden ground, as the abode of the enemies of our country. It was extraordinary. They absolutely had houses, churches, streets, fields and children!' We had suffered somewhat from intellectual inbreeding and were surfeited by insularity. Fortunately, and perhaps as the obverse of our isolation, we possessed an extremely vigorous tradition of native intelligence. The two great seminal minds of the age (the phrase was coined by John Stuart Mill in 1838) were both deeply impregnated by European ideas: Jeremy Bentham by Gallic empiricism, S. T. Coleridge by German idealism: yet both carried on vigorous native traditions at the same time— Bentham and his disciples that of Locke, and Coleridge that of the seventeenth-century English Platonists.

In literature, as in philosophy, and especially in poetry, England led the world from her own sources of both inspiration and achievement. She had created and sustained the novel almost single-handed, and it was within the short span of the Regency that two of its greatest exponents, Walter Scott and

Jane Austen, brought their art to its highest level of achievement. Painting, with Lawrence and Turner, Wilkie and Constable, Blake and Palmer, Bonington and Cotman, was still at the high tide which had been flowing since the days of Gainsborough and Reynolds. Among the fine arts, only music and the drama were in eclipse, as they had been for long and were long to remain. Where England shone in the early years of the nineteenth century, she shone effulgent. Truly, 'great spirits on earth were sojourning . . . standing apart upon the forehead of the age to come.' Keats meant the poets, and truly it was a time almost unparalleled for poetry, and certainly unparalleled for the tragedy of poets. The age to come was quickly to be robbed of its inheritance. Before the death of George IV, England had lost Keats, Shelley, and Byron. It was a tragedy that had begun before these latter-days of fatality. Coleridge had dried up of great poetry before 1800, and Wordsworth was to write little that we care to remember after it. Was it something in the air of the nineteenth century as it advanced that was unfit for the English poets to breathe? Tuberculosis, laudanum, sheer fatality, had most to do with it. Certainly, another great age of prose was at the dawn, and of the opposite of poetry (as Coleridge insisted)—science.

The Regency not only saw the novel of manners and the historical novel at their greatest in Jane Austen and Walter Scott;

Sir Walter Scott

it gave birth to a galaxy of novelists whom we remember, rather naturally, as Victorians. The births included Thackeray (1811), Dickens (1812), Trollope (1815), Charlotte Brontë (1816), Emily Brontë (1818), George Eliot (1819). Mrs Gaskell (1810), Charles Reade (1814) and Charles Kingsley (1819) might be added. Despite, indeed because of, the year of their birth, there would be no point in describing any of

152

them as Regency novelists. And yet, as Walter Allen has pointed out, they share a certain climate of ideas and feelings, a set of fundamental assumptions, which writers of a slightly later birth— Samuel Butler (1835), Meredith (1828), Hardy (1840)—were to question, even if the reading public still took them for granted. They share the flavour, or the hang-over, of the England of George IV. The novelists who were actually producing novels in those years, however (apart from Sir Walter and Miss Austen), were a pretty commonplace lot. John Galt's *Annals of the Parish* came out in 1813, and is mainly memorable for suggesting 'Utilitarian' as a party name to John Stuart Mill. There was Miss Edgeworth ('The Great Maria'), Mrs Radcliffe, Letitia Landon, and a few more whose books were widely read,

Jane Austen

and yet were really survivors from the turn of the century. And in the late 'twenties there were new names coming to the fore: Disraeli with *Vivian Grey* (1826) and Bulwer Lytton with *Pelham* (1828), which were soon to be famous. But the great spate of novels which came out while George, Prince of Wales, was Regent, amounted only to what we should now describe as pulp. There was an enormous output of rubbish, highly popular and profitable rubbish. For sheer output in terms of quantity, as distinct from quality, few periods can rival the Regency. Perhaps it is too much to expect more than two novelists of genius to be at work in so short a period of time. What is remarkable is the fact that the others were so generally inferior.

The fact is that there was now a reading public. Half a century earlier, Dr Johnson had announced that we were 'a reading nation'. He had also expressed his gratification at being able to concur with the 'common reader'. This manifestly meant that there was a high average of taste among those who habitually read books. Things had changed. There was now a large and undiscriminating public for an inferior form of

153

fiction. People still read the classics of English literature: Bunyan, Defoe, Addison; the great novelists of the previous age, Richardson, Fielding, Sterne and Smollett; they read the great essayists, Johnson himself, and the general writers, like Goldsmith. But they had a ravenous appetite also for Mrs Gore's *Manners of the Day*, Mrs Bruton's *Self-control*, Mrs Radcliffe's *Romance of the Forest*. Most of all they had a passion for the products of Mr Lane's Minerva Press in Leadenhall Street. William Lane had founded a circulating library alongside his press, and such was the demand for the *Minerva Novels* that he quickly made a large fortune and was to be seen riding about London in a carriage-and-four with footmen and cockades. Mostly his novels came out in three volumes in mottled covers, and were written by ladies who described themselves as 'Mrs' this and that. The tales of horror were in especial demand. The titles remind one of lower-class science fiction of today: *The Demon of Sicily*, *The Mysterious Hand* and *Subterranean Horrors*, by disciples of Mrs Radcliffe of *Mysteries of Udolpho* fame. Mrs Mary Meake and a tribe of scribblers of feeble romance produced *Midnight Weddings* (highly successful), and such titles as *The Miraculous Nuptials* and *Bewildered Affections*, while for the glamorous hero there was *Thaddeus of Warsaw*, and for fainting-fits *Santo Sebastiano*. It was hardly possible for even the satirists to invent titles too absurd. The lending libraries— which started up in provincial towns and watering-places in large numbers — supplemented Mr Lane's premises in Leadenhall Street in order to meet the insatiable demand; for people carried them off a score at a time, and the average price to buy such works was thirty shillings or

'*Tales of horror*'

A London bookshop: Sam's, Royal Library, in Bond Street

more. Mrs Barnett's *The Beggar Girl and her Benefactors*, in seven volumes, sold 2,000 copies at *36s.* on the day of publication. The existence of this tasteless appetite for what Coleridge called 'desultory reading', was a phenomenon that came in for many and severe strictures from critics of public taste. When he wrote his *Biographia Literaria* (1817), Coleridge himself declined to compliment the 'pass-time', or the kill-time, of the devotees of the circulating libraries with the name of 'reading'. He preferred to call it 'a kind of Beggarly daydreaming', of the same genus with gaming, swinging on a gate, spitting over a bridge, smoking or taking snuff.

As usual, the disease was far less malignant than the critics made out. Nor was it confined to the half-educated or the merely idle. Reading Minerva novels was indulged in by every class of reader, rather as crosswords were to be at a later time. People read them to mock and to laugh as well as to engage mind (sic) and imagination. Mary Lamb and Mary Russell Mitford and the young Tom Macaulay consumed them in large quantities. So did the Austen family, for a time. Jane herself sampled them, found them generally a bore, and turned to satirising the taste in novels of her own. *Northanger Abbey* was published in 1818, after the authoress' death. But it was written in 1797 and 1798, when the *Mysteries of Udolpho* was all the rage. The satire was good for at least twenty years. As a novel it transcends its time, and will be read when *Udolpho* is forgotten.

Standards of criticism, quite apart from satire and raillery, had been rising from the beginning of the century. The *Edinburgh Review* had been set on foot in 1801, the *Quarterly* followed in 1808, while magazines like *Blackwood's*, the *London Magazine*, the *Examiner* and the *Westminster Review* were all in train over the next twenty years. All had their devotees, so gargantuan was the taste for periodical literature. The father and mother of the family was undoubtedly the *Edinburgh* in its blue and buff covers, the colour scheme of Whiggery. It cost 5*s.* (6*s.* after 1808), and it was selling 13,000 copies in 1813, as compared with 1,500 in the first year of publication twelve years earlier. Francis Jeffrey, the editor, reckoned that each copy was seen by at least three readers. The Review was addressed to the educated middle classes. Indeed, it helped to create what has been called *l'homme moyen intellectuel*: the reader who could and would read articles on scholarly and scientific subjects without needing to have everything explained to him. By paying his contributors top prices and maintaining anonymity for their work, he raised the standards and the prestige of reviewing beyond all previous knowledge. Instead of 'abstracts' from new books, often insignificant, the *Edinburgh* produced well-reasoned analyses of worth-while literature, often running to 15 or 20 pages. With the trash ignored and the rest reviewed seriously, there was little excuse for anyone to imagine that Mr Lane's Library represented in any respect the literary standards of Regency England. S. T. Coleridge, who had often spoken of newspaper reviewing—especially when anonymous—as beneath contempt—came to pay his tribute to the *Edinburgh* when he wrote *Biographia Literaria* in 1817. 'I think the commencement of the *Edinburgh Review* an important epoch in periodical criticism; and that it has a claim upon the gratitude of the literary republic, and indeed of the reading public at large, for having originated the scheme of reviewing those books only which are susceptible and deserving of argumentative criticism', and leaving the trash or mediocrity to sink into oblivion by its own weight.

The avidity of the reading public for Minerva novels was simply one aspect of the appetite for marvels in an age of startling events and transformation scenes. Nothing that was going on at that time could rival the miraculous achievements of science, and particularly of chemistry. Europe had gone up in smoke, and the demon king of the cannon had lately vanished away to an island in the wastes of the Atlantic. But at the Royal Institution in Albemarle Street there had appeared a resident magician in young Humphry Davy from Devonshire, the chemical genius of the age, administering laughing-gas from a silken bag for the delectation of fashionable mixed audiences. 'Fashion and chemistry', said Francis Horner, the eminent political economist, after hearing Davy lecture to 300 fashionables, 'form a very incongruous union'. The installation of private boxes in the lecture-theatre, however, was the idea of the Treasurer, not of Davy, and it was nobody's fault if chemistry was a sensational form of science, replete with bangs and smells and bright lights. The laughing-gas was a furore. Poets and painters, potters and antiquaries, statesmen and

Humphry Davy (right) assisting at a lecture in the Royal Institution

popular novelists, Maria Edgeworth and Isaac D'Israeli and Josiah Wedgwood, everyone who was anyone might insert his or her nose in the silken bag and record his or her sensations. It afforded all the pleasures of alcohol or laudanum at next-to-nothing a sniff, without unpleasant after-effects. In an age of Minerva novels and all the rhapsodic nonsense of romanticism, it was sublime.

Davy was knighted by the Prince Regent in 1812. His career was the scientific romance of the Regency, eminently typical of its time and place. He is remembered for the invention of the miner's safety-lamp. At the age of 42 he was elected President of the Royal Society. He married a rich wife, and died in 1829, leaving a Testament to his countrymen under the title of *Consolations of Travel, or the Last Days of a Philosopher*. He began his career with a bag of laughing-gas, and ended it with a book of very gassy philosophy. Yet Coleridge said that if he had not been the first chemist, he would have been the first poet of his age. He remains interesting for the safety-lamp, and for his gifts as a populariser of science. It was what the age demanded: science in simple terms, preferably with ocular demonstrations. The Continent was closed by war, and as his brother John remarked: 'whatever diverted the public mind and afforded new objects for contemplation, pure and independent sources of amusement and gratification, must have been very welcome.'

'People have nowadays got a strange opinion that everything should be taught by lectures . . .', Dr Johnson had once observed. This certainly seemed to be true of the English when the war was over. By 1815, London was fairly humming with lectures. The newspapers announced courses on everything from literature to electrolysis. Nor was this multiplicity of interest, especially in science, frivolous or sensation-seeking alone. People were becoming aware that the advancement of science was to be a mighty factor in the national fortunes in industry and agriculture. Among the earliest tasks which the Managers of the Royal Institution proposed to Humphry Davy after his election to its Chair of Chemistry were the chemistry of tanning, the analysis of minerals, and the application of chemistry to agriculture. Davy insisted on the utilitarian value of science in his inaugural lecture. He expatiated on the beneficent alliance between the man of science and the manufacturer, and on the union of enlightenment and happiness. 'We do not look to distant ages', he concluded. 'We look for a time that we may reasonably expect—FOR A BRIGHT DAY, OF WHICH WE ALREADY BEHOLD THE DAWN.' Even Coleridge, friend and admirer of Davy, though he suspected the habit of

Humphry Davy, with his miner's lamp

casting pearls before swine, was prepared to join in, now. In the winter of 1817, on Monday and Thursday evenings, he dispensed brilliantly, if somewhat irregularly, at the *Crown and Anchor* in the Strand, courses on literature and philosophy. He wished, he said, to increase his utility. He was, too, rather more than usually hard-up. It may be doubted whether the lectures were ever really popular, but the tone of his prospectus laid stress on the intellectual needs of the common man. He wanted to convey, he said, those rules and principles of sound judgment which men engaged in business and the active duties of the world could hardly be expected to attain for themselves. He would show 'how moderate a number of volumes, judiciously chosen, would suffice for the attainment of every wise and desirable purpose'. He would offer 'a few easy rules for the attainment of a manly, unaffected and pure language' for writing, oratory and conversation. He proposed an outline of medieval history, and a series on great men of letters. In fact, the leading mind of the age was prepared to lend itself to the cause of that popularisation of culture which he deplored elsewhere as leading to its 'plebification'.

Two years later, Leigh Hunt founded *The Indicator, or Knowledge for All*, a cheap journal aimed at 'the Common Reader', a pioneer publication in the cause of 'outlines of

Leigh Hunt

everything'. In 1827, Henry Brougham founded the Society for the Diffusion of Useful Knowledge, or, as Thomas Love Peacock called it, 'The Steam Intellect Society'. It put forth sixpenny text-books on every conceivable subject, preferably science. England had entered the age of *The Penny Magazine*, *The Penny Encyclopedia* and *The Library of Entertaining Knowledge*. It was at this time that Henry Crabb Robinson fell in with a master bricklayer, 'whose appearance was that of a very low person', who turned out to be 'enlightened by those principles of political economy which are indeed becoming common. . . . He did not talk of the books of Adam Smith, but seemed imbued with their spirit.' Mr Robinson marvelled that such ideas had descended 'on the hod and trowel'. No doubt his fellow-traveller had been reading the sixpenny *Illustrations of Political Economy* which Miss Martineau was putting forth from the Useful Knowledge Society by the later 'twenties, with enormous success.

How, it may be asked, was Mr Robinson's bricklayer able to read Miss Martineau's tracts? How is Samuel Bamford able to avow, of the years 1815 and 1816, that 'at this time the writings of William Cobbett suddenly became of great authority; they were read on nearly every cottage hearth in the manufacturing districts. . . .' Why had a cheap edition of Tom Paine's *Rights of Man* at once led to a trial for sedition? Why in 1819 did Government impose a heavy stamp-duty on newspapers? To judge from statements about the extent of illiteracy among the poor in Victorian England, it might be imagined that elementary education was either non-existent or extremely ineffective in the earlier years of the century. In fact, however, those years saw some of the most energetic and widespread movements to promote the schooling (not, perhaps, the education) of the poor. These efforts were made by private enterprise, and nearly always as a part of charitable endeavour, or rescue work among the children of the poor. The Charity School movement, to get waifs and strays and abandoned children into schools where they could be trained to some useful occupation (generally some form of domestic service for girls) had been on foot under private subscription for 100 years. With the growth of more populous towns, respectable citizens and property-owners (and everyone who wanted a quiet Sunday) had taken to various efforts to get unruly children off the streets for at least one day in the week. The great Sunday School movement, which was to achieve amazing results, at least in terms of numbers, during the first half of the nineteenth century (and beyond) sprang from Robert Raikes' work for the rowdy children of Gloucester. As soon as it became manifest that private endeavour could solve the problem of Sunday schools, the notion spread that the day-school problem might be solved in the same way. Joseph Lancaster opened his school in Borough Road, Southwark, in 1798: here, some 100 boys and girls were taught mechanics, reading, writing, and arithmetic at about fourpence a week per head. His success led quickly to the formation of the Royal Lancastrian Society, and by 1814 there had come into existence the British and Foreign Schools Society to co-ordinate the voluntary work of a multitude of subscribers to the cause.

harity School in Gravel Lane, London, originally founded for Protestant dissenters

Primary-school education for girls

Lancaster was primarily a humanitarian, neither a politician nor an educationalist. His aim was to keep the children busy and happy. He marched them about, and he ran discipline by means of medals and rituals, so that punishment by beating and other forms of severity was unnecessary. But politics, in the form of religious politics, very soon entered in. For he provided an undenominational form of religious instruction, and was quickly suspected of furthering infidelity—at that time regarded as the twin sister of sedition. A rival Society, the 'National Society for promoting the Education of the Poor in the Principles of the Established Church' was established, likewise a voluntary organisation, but nourished by the funds and the energies of squire and parson and the establishment in general. The rivalry between British schools and National schools was obstructive by the time (in the 1830s) when the State began to grant funds, but it served to multiply the grand total of schools set up in these busy years. Regency England saw the foundation of primary education on a basis at once voluntary, denominational, and—above all—cheap. It had little to do with education, only with schooling, or elementary instruction in the three Rs. It took the edge off the latent savagery of a child-population exposed to the worst influences of an increasingly urban and industrial society. It was a prophylactic.

Adam Smith, in *The Wealth of Nations* (1776), had foreseen the necessity of schools in an industrial society. 'The man whose whole life is spent in performing a few simple operations, of which the effects, too, are perhaps always the same, has no occasion to exert his understanding, or to exercise his invention, in finding out expedients for removing difficulties which never occur. He naturally loses therefore the habit of such exertions, and generally becomes as stupid and ignorant as it is possible for a human creature to become.' Although he liked to protest

162

that he never could make out what 'the old Scotch tax-gatherer'
was talking about, Cobbett agreed that 'schools are very
proper things in many cases: in large cities and towns . . .',
where the natural education which comes from a country environment is to seek. 'I do know', he concludes, 'that I myself
was at work in the fields before I was six. And this was
"education", properly so called. Education means rearing-up,
not teaching to read and write.' In short, education has to be
institutionalised when life becomes mechanised.

Unfortunately, but not surprisingly, education became
mechanised, too. Working on the maxim 'What a boy can
learn, a boy can teach', a great mechanical invention appeared.
It was called the Monitorial method. No one ever made out a
convincing title to the patent, though the disciples of both
Lancaster and the Rev. Andrew Bell, his rival of the National
Society, fought over it for years. It amounted to this: the master
taught the boys, and then the boys—or the older and abler of
them—taught the other boys. The proceedings were organised
in small groups of monitors and pupils, scattered about the
floor of the school room. Every stage was marked by the
ringing of a large hand-bell. Every lesson started and stopped

Public-school education: the school room at Eton

like a stage in a process by a large human machine. And it all
cost next to nothing. Just under 7s. 6d. per annum per pupil,
Lancaster said. In an age and a society living at the dawn of
large-scale mechanised industry, mass-production in the school
was a recognisable form of progress. The monitorial schools
were the latest wonder to visit and to admire. 'This incomparable machine,' Coleridge called the system, 'this vast moral
steam-engine.' It was 'an especial gift of Providence to the
human race,' in so far, of course, as it was in the hands of Dr
Bell and the Established Church, and—again—so long as we
did not imagine that it, of itself, formed an efficient national
education. For a long time people imagined just this, and that
our educational problems were solved. In fact, it was another
branch of the Steam Intellect Society.

The few who thought at all deeply about the problem of
national education realised that reform must begin at the top,
in the universities and great schools, where standards were
set, where the teachers were produced, and whose influence
could deeply permeate the rest of society. During the first thirty
years of the nineteenth century, the universities were developing
a more rigorous system of examinations. The Senate House
Examinations had been instituted at Cambridge in the mid-
eighteenth century, supplementing and steadily replacing the
ancient disputatory, or *viva voce* contests. At Oxford, the

The London University, designed by William Wilkins, 1827–8

Public Examination Statute was passed in 1800. Largely under the influence of Bentham and his disciples, the University of London was established in the 1820s, and incorporated by Charter in 1836: a pioneer of the modern university, with its scope for useful learning. Pioneers of reform in the Public Schools were entering upon the labours which were to transform, and save, the old schools throughout the course of the nineteenth century. Dr Butler was at Shrewsbury by 1798, and Thomas Arnold became headmaster of Rugby in 1828.

The bodies as well as the minds of the people were in the course of salvation. There was a great decline in the incidence of venereal disease, Francis Place tells us, due to greater sobriety and improvement of morals following upon the Wesleyan and Evangelical movements. Cheap cotton shirts, more and better fresh vegetables, more rapid transport, were all on the side of improved standards of public health. There was much to do, however. The outbreak of Asiatic cholera in 1831, brought about by infected drinking-water, left a frightful sense of unavoidable fatality.

It is evident that many of the characteristic features of English life that we associate with the Victorian Age were already showing themselves when the Prince Regent, having reigned for ten years as King George IV, died in 1830. The all-pervading feature is, of course, the change to a mood which might be called one of moral seriousness. It is not simply that by 1830 powder and rouge had gone out of fashion or that men were wearing stove-pipe hats and sober broadcloth more commonly than the plumage of the Regency dandies, or even that there was an increasing public for the works of Thomas Bowdler. It was rather that a multitudinous society, concerned with great enterprises and acute social problems, was becoming more and more aware that it simply could not afford trifling, waste and dilettantism, but must evolve and observe high and serious standards of both public and private behaviour. The celebrated 'high seriousness' of the Victorians was indeed one aspect of men and women oppressed, but not depressed, by the delicate and complicated problems of a society which threatened to outstrip their capacity for controlling it. Most notable as a symptom of such concern was the growth of respect for professionalism, and of organisations by which professional men sought to set and maintain standards. Nothing could be more apposite to this movement than the foundation of the Society (1771) and then the Institute (1818) of Civil Engineers, by the men who were building the roads and bridges—and soon railways—into the future.

The amateur was giving way to the professional in everything from school-teaching to cricket, from civil engineering to the civil service. The Inspector was becoming a characteristic figure in every walk of society, often resented, but steadily intruding, more especially after the spate of reformist legislation that followed the passing of the Great Reform Bill of 1832. Inspection as a means of securing enforcement was integral to success. By the 1830s Bentham with his cult of rational government, rationally administered, had won. By 1824 there was even a Royal Society for the Prevention of Cruelty to Animals.

The girl who came to the throne in 1837 was in many respects a daughter of the Regency. She was born in the year of Peterloo, and the world around her was still that of the ageing Prinny. When she was seven she went down to Windsor to meet her uncle. As Lytton Strachey described the encounter: 'The old rip, bewigged and gouty, ornate and enormous, with his jewelled mistress by his side and his flaunting court about him, received the tiny creature who was one day to hold in those same halls a very different state. "Give me your little paw", he said; and two ages touched.' In girlhood, as the young Queen of England, she was in love with 'Dear Lord M.' Melbourne had been a crony of the Prince and a habitué of Carlton House in his young days. When Prince Albert at length replaced Lord M. in Victoria's affections, he was dismayed and disconcerted by a vestigial Regency trait of his bride: the passion for dancing all night and dashing out to see the sun rise over London. She had at first little sympathy with her husband's wish to spend his evenings with learned men discussing serious subjects. However the Prince Consort triumphed in the end, and perhaps

166

much that we think of as Victorian could better be called Albertian. All the same, the people over whom the Queen ruled had been prepared for the Victorian Age by such emergent features of Regency England as Utilitarianism, Evangelicalism, Malthusian economics, and the monitorial schools.

The Age of Seriousness, for better or for worse, had dawned.

Further Reading

J. W. Adamson, *History of English Education*
Walter Allen, *The English Novel*
John Clive, *Scotch Reviewers*
Muriel Jaeger, *Before Victoria*
Chester W. New, *Life of Henry Brougham, to 1830*
Sir Harold Nicolson, *Good Behaviour*
C. M. Norrie, *Bridging the Years*
Anne Treneer, *The Mercurial Chemist, A Life of Sir Humphry Davy*

Index

The numerals in heavy type refer to the page numbers of the illustrations

Academies, **47, 123**, 124
Actors and acting, 78
Adams, Parson, 141
Addington, Dr, 59
Addington, Henry, *see* Sidmouth, Viscount
Addison, Joseph, 154
Addison, W., *English Spas*, 136
Age of Seriousness, the Dawn of the, Chap IX
Agriculture, 22, **23, 24, 25, 26**, 27
Albert, Prince, 166
Alexander I, Czar of Russia, 83
Allen, Walter, 152, 153
American Revolution, 141
Apprentices, recruitment of parish, 35
Architecture, 7, **8**, 55, **56**, 64, 65–9, **71–3, 117, 119, 120, 123**, 143, **144**
Argyle Rooms, **80**
Aristocracy, *see* Upper classes
Arkwright, Richard, 31
Armchair, **126**
Army, 59
Arnold, Dr Thomas (of Rugby), 165
Assembly Rooms, 128, 131
Astley's Circus, 79
Austen, Jane, 96, 121, 124, 152, **153**
    Emma, 57–9, 107
    Northanger Abbey, 134, 155
    Persuasion, 19
    Sanditon, 129, 135
    Sense and Sensibility, 136

Bailey, *Festus*, 143
Balls, **58**, 59, **80**
Bamford, Samuel, 59, 63, 88, 97, 99, 160
    Passages in the Life of a Radical, 36–40
Bank of England, **75**
Barclay's Brewery, 76
Barnett, Mrs, *The Beggar Girl and Her Benefactors*, 155
Barry, Sir Charles (architect), 118
Barrymore, Lord, 102

Bath, 128, 131
    Pump Room, 134
Bathing, sea, **129, 130**
Beckford, William, 105, 143
Beddoes, Thomas (poet), 143
Beggar's Opera, 84
Belcher (prize-fighter), 110
Bell, Rev. Andrew, 163, 164
Ben (prize-fighter), 111
Benenden, Kent, 147
Bennett, Arnold, 32
Bentham, Jeremy, and the Benthamites, 84, 91, **92, 93, 94**, 151, 165
Berners, Isopel, 4
Bewick, Thomas, 30
Birkbeck, George, 30
Birmingham, 34, 64
Blackamoor's Head, Nottingham, 143
Blacksmiths, 2, **17**
Blackwood's Magazine, 156
Blake, William, 152
Blunt, Wilfred Scawen, *The Old Squire* (quoted), 51
Bolton, Lancashire, **40**
Bonington, Richard Parkes, 152
Borrow, George, 4, 18, 100
    Lavengro, 18, 60, 109, 110
    Romany Rye, 18
Botham, Samuel, 127
Bournemouth, 133
Bowdler, Thomas, *Family Shakespeare*, 142, 165
Boxing, *see* Prize-fighting
Brandreth, Jeremiah, 97, **98**
Bricklaying, **32**
Bridgewater, Duke of, 56
Bridlington Bay, **129**
Brighton, 132
    Chain Pier, **132, 133**
    Royal Pavilion, **107**, 118
Brindley, James, 12, 56
Bristol, 64
British and Foreign Schools Society, 161
British Museum, 76, 118
Brodribb, John, 114

169

Brontë Sisters, 152
Brougham, Henry, Lord, 30, 88, 92, 148, 160
Broughton (prize-fighter), 111
Brown Bear, The, Haymarket, 81
Brummell, Beau, 6, 91, 105
Brunel, Sir Mark, 13, 91, 135
Bruton, Mrs, *Self Control*, 154
Buck, A., 109
Buckingham Palace, 70
Bull and Mouth, Piccadilly, **4, 5, 11, 13**
Burdett, Sir Francis, 50, 53, 88, 92, **96**, 97, 98, 105
Burke, Edmund, 44, 56, 99
Burke, Thomas, *Murder at Elstree*, 110
Burlington Arcade, **48**
Burton, Decimus, **66**
Bury, *The Angel* at, 11
Business, 8
Butler, Dr Samuel (Head of Shrewsbury School), 165
Butler, Samuel (author), 153
Byron, Lord, 91, 103, 143, 152

Calico printer, **29**, 30
Camberwell, 16
Cambridge, 94, 118, 121, 142, 164
  Senate House Examinations at, 164
Canals, 12, **13**
Canaletto, 62
Canning, George, 9, 86, 88
Card games, 126, **127**
Carlton House, 68, 70, 90, 93
Carlyle, Thomas, 22, 45, 140
Caroline, Queen, 132, 145
Carriages, **2**, **73, 74, 114**
Cartwright, Major John, 94, 97, 98
Cartwright, Mr (dentist), 59
Castlereagh, Robert Stewart, Viscount, 9, **86**, 88, 89
Cato Street Conspiracy, 13, 96, 99, **100**
Census, 3
Charing Cross, 81, 93
Charity School Movement, 160, **161**
Charleys (night watchmen), **82**
Charlotte, Princess, 132
Chartist Movement, 36
Cheltenham, **128, 135**
Children, education of, 47, 114, **123**
  employment of, 35, **37**, 141
  pastimes of, 122, **125**
Cholera epidemic (1831), 165
Church, the, 60, 141, 143ff.
  building, 143, **144**
Church Building Act (*1818*), 143

Civil Engineers, Society and Institution of, 166
Clapham Sect (Evangelists), 145, 146, 147
Clapham, Sir John, 32
Clare College, Cambridge, 142
Clergymen, **60**
Clerkenwell, watch-making at, 33
Clothes, children's, **122, 124, 125, 149**
  lower class, 21, **22, 23**
  middle class, **46, 48, 49**
  upper class, 2–7, **9, 10, 13, 50, 57, 58, 59, 102, 103, 105, 115, 124, 125, 126, 155**
  women's, **103, 114, 116, 121, 124, 127, 154**
Clough, Arthur Hugh, *Dipsychus*, 45
Coal gas lighting, **78**
Coal Hole, the Strand, 81
Coal-mining, 29, 30, 34, **35, 39**, 147
Cobbett, William, 5, 10, 17, 22, 23, 26, 27, 54, 55, 63, **95**, 98, 99, **101**, 117, 138, 146, **147**, 159, 160, 163
Cock, The, Haymarket, 81
Cock-fighting, **10**
Coke, Thomas (of Holkham), 53, 56
Coleridge, S. T., 27, 45, 46, 89, 141, 151
  Biographia Literaria, 155, 156
Coliseum, the, Regent's Park, **66**
Collins, Wilkie, *The Moonstone*, 148
Colquhoun, Patrick, *Resources of the British Empire*, 7
Commerce, 8, **44, 45, 48, 49**
Constable, John, R.A., 152
Conyngham, Lady, 107
Copestake, Mr (of Uttoxeter), 34
Corinthian, the, 102, 109
Corn, 24–7
Corruption, 111, 112, 114
Corsets for men, 103, **108**
Cotman, John Sell, 152
Cottage industry, 36–**8**
Cotton, 33, 35, **36**
Courtesans, 80, **103, 114**
Covent Garden Theatre, 79
Coventry, 34
Cowper, William, 135
Craftsmanship, 4, 6, 15, **16**
Craven, Earl of, 115
Craven's Head, 81
Crawley, Sir Pitt, 53
Crawley, Rawdon, 139
Creevey, Mr, 107
Cribb, Tom (prize-fighter), 110
Cricket, **111–13**

Criminals and Crime prevention, 19, 82, **83**, **84**
Crockford, 111
Crockford's Club, 79, **80**
Cromer, 134
Crowley, Abraham, 34
Crown and Anchor, Strand, 159
Cruelty, 10, 11, 18
 Royal Society for the Prevention of, 166
Cubitt, 69
Cumberland Terrace, **71**
Cyprians (courtesans), 80, **103**, **114**, **115**

Dancing, **58**, 59, 80, 103, **104**
Dandy, the, **102**
Darnall, professional cricket at, 112
Darwin, Erasmus, 64
Davy, Sir Humphry, **157–9**
 Consolations of Travel, 158
Davy, John (quoted), 158
Debden, Church of St Mary and All Saints at, 120
Defoe, Daniel, 15, 154
 Robinson Crusoe, 142
Denham, Sir Edward, 135
Denmark Hill, 16
Derby, 64
Derbyshire Rising (the Pentrich Revolution), 98
Derriman, Festus, 53
Dickens, Charles, 6, 19, 32, 95, 152
 Our Mutual Friend, 18, 142
 Pickwick, 9, 12, 18
'Dippers' (bathing attendants), 133
Disraeli, Benjamin, 85, 87
 The Spirit of Whiggism, 43
 Vivian Grey, 153
D'Israeli, Isaac, 158
Dissenters, 46, 60, **160**
Domestic servants, 32, **33**, 127, 140
Dorchester, Oxfordshire, 136
Downing College, Cambridge, 118
Duelling, **9**
Dulwich, Soane's Art Gallery and Mausoleum at, 75
Durham, 34

Eardley-Wilmot, Sir John, 53
Earthquakes, 140
Edgeworth, Maria, 66, 153, 158
Edinburgh, 64
Edinburgh Review, 148, 156

Education, adult, 30
 Charity school, 160–2
 Children's, 47, 114, **123**, 124, 160–2
 Monitorial system, 163, 164
 Public school, **163**, 165
 Sunday school, **149**, 161
Egremont, Lord, 156
Egyptian Hall, Piccadilly, **65**
Eldon, John Scott, Lord, 89, **90**
Elegance, **7**
Elephant and Castle, The, 11
Eliot, George, 152
Enclosures, 16
Endsleigh (landscape gardener), 6
Endsleigh Cottage, Milton Abbot, **119**
English Platonists, 151
Entertainment, **10**, **18**, **28**, **57**, **79–82**, **126**, **127**
Eton School Room, **163**
Euston (Norfolk), 141
Evangelical Revival, 139–**41**, 145
Examiner, The, 156
Executions, public, 19, **83**, **84**

Factory Act (1818), 35
Factory children, 141
Family prayers, 140
Farmers, farmhouses, 23, **24**, **27**, **28**
'Fashionable Impures' (courtesans), **80**, **103**, **114**, **115**
Felix, Mr, 114
Felkin, William, *History of Machine-wrought hosiery and Lace Manufacture*, 37
Fielding, Henry, 154
Fitzgerald, Pamela (quoted), 104
Fives Court, St Martin's Street, Sparring at the, **109**
Flaming Tinman, the (pugilist), 4
Fletcher, Mrs Sarah, Epitaph of, 136
Floyer and Barnard, *History of Cold Bathing*, 130
Foundry workers, **22**
Fox-hunting, 53, 54
French Revolution, 94, 140, 141, 143
Furniture, **7**, **26**, **28**, **46**, **57**, **58**, 105, **121**, **124**, 125, **126**

Gainsborough, Thomas, 64, 152
Galt, John, *Annals of the Parish*, 153
Gambling, **10**, 79, **80**, 114
Game Laws, **52**, **53**
Games, children's, **125**
Gardener, **6**
Gaskell, Mrs, 152

Gas lighting, 78
Gasman, the (prize-fighter), 110
Gas Works, **78**
General Post Office, 118
Gentleman, The Country, 50, **51**
Gentleman's Magazine (quoted), 120
George III, 1, 103, 133, 142
George IV, 104, 105, **106**, 107, **108**, 132, 165, **167**
George, The, Southwark, 11
Gibbon, E., *Decline and Fall of the Roman Empire,* 142
'Gigmanity', 140
Gillray (cartoonist), 102
Girls, education of, 123, 124, **162**
Gloucester, 161
Goldsmith, Oliver, 154
    History of England, 124
Gore, Mrs, *Manners of the Day,* 154
Gothic Revival, 55, **56**, 87, 118, **119**, **120**, **144**
Grafton, Duke of, 141
Gray's *Microcosm* (quoted), 6, 10, 11
Greek Revival, **75**, 118
Gronow, Captain, *Memoirs,* 102
Grove House, Regent's Park, **67**
Gurney's steam carriage, **15**

Hambledon cricketers, 111
Hardy, Thomas, 4, 153
    Jude the Obscure, 25
Harley Family, 104
Harris, David, 111
Harrogate, 131
Harrowby, Lord, 100
Hats, 21
Haydon, Benjamin Robert, 45, 56, 64, 151
Hazlitt, William, 3, 60, 92, 110, 148
Health, 17
Hell Fire Club, 141
Heron, Sir Robert, 53
Highgate Archway, Construction of, **14**
Hoadley, Bishop Benjamin, 141
Hobby-horse, 14, **15**
Hodgskin, Thomas, 30
Holcroft, Tom, 3, 12
Holkham Hall, Norfolk, 53, 56
Homosexuality, 104, 105
Horner, Francis (quoted), 157
Horses, **2**, **3**, **11–13**, 25
House, Humphry, *The Dickens World* (quoted), 18
House parties, 128
Housing, **23**, **24**, 27, 28, 31, 37
    London middle class, **68**
    London upper class, **65**, 71, **72**, **73**

Howitt, Mary, 143
Howitt, Thomas, colliery manager, **30**
Howitt, William, *The Boys' Country Book,* 30, 40, 122, 137, 143
Hoy (passenger ship), 135, **136**
Hucknall Church, Nottinghamshire, Byron's burial at, 143
Hungerford, 110
Hunt, Henry ('Orator'), 39, 50, 98, **99**
Hunt, Leigh, 146, 159, **160**
Huntingdon, Selina, Countess of, 141
Hussey, Christopher, *The Picturesque,* 137
Hyde Park, **74**

Indicator, The, or Knowledge for All, 159
Industry, growth of large-scale, 29
Infant mortality, 17
Inns, **4**, **5**, 11, **12**
Interior decoration, 125, **126**
Ipswich, *The White Hart* at, 11
Irish immigrants, 29
Irving, Sir Henry, 78, 114

Jay, Rev. William, 60
Jeffrey, Francis, 148, 156
Johnson, Dr Samuel, 119, 154, 158

Keats, John, 152
Kedleston, 119
Kingsley, Charles, 152
Knight, Payne, *Analytical Enquiry into the Principles of Taste,* 118
Knightley, Mr, 134

Labelye, Charles, 62
Labourer, country, 22, **23**, **25**
    housing, **23**, 24
    food, 25, **26**
    wages, 24
Labourer, town, 29ff., **32**, **35**, **37**
Ladies at home, 121
    of fashion, 80, **114**, **115**
Lamb, Mary, 155
Lancaster, Joseph, 161, 162
Landon, Letitia, 153
Landscape gardening, **6**, 8
Lane, William (publisher), 154, 156
Langley, Batty, 121
Law, William, *Serious call to a devout and holy Life,* 141
Lawrence, D. H., 4, 40
Lawrence, Sir Thomas, R.A., 64, 152

Leamington Spa, 128
Lewis, C. S., 19
Libraries, 133, **134**, 154, **155**
Library of Entertaining Knowledge, 160
Lieven, Princess de, 107
Linen-draper's shop, **49**
Lisbon Earthquake, 140
Literary criticism, 156
Literature, 148, 151ff.
Liverpool, Robert Jenkinson, Earl of, 85, 86, 89, 90, 143, 144
Liverpool, Wesleyan Chapel at, **139**
Locke, John, 151
London, **4, 5, 11, 13, 45, 48**, Chap. IV, **63, 65–9, 71**, 140
  bookshop, **155**
  Charity Schools, **161**
  Church building in, 143, **144**
  Corresponding Society, 94
  the spread of, 16, 63
  University, **164**, 165
London Magazine, 156
Looms, hand, **16**
  power, 33, **34**
Lord's Cricket Ground, 111
Loudon, John Claudius (landscape gardener), 6
Lower classes, the, **3, 6, 14, 16–19**, Chap. II
Luscombe, near Dawlish, **120**
Lyme Regis, 128
Lytton, Bulwer, *Pelham*, 133

Macadam, John Loudon, 10
Macaulay, Thomas, 155
Mail coaches, 10, **12, 13**
Malthus, Thomas, *Essay on the Principles of Population*, 138
'Man and Flag Act' (1864), 14
Manchester, 33, 34, **36**, 39, **93**, 140
Manners and morals, Chap. VI
Man-trap, 'Humane', **53**
Margate, 135
  Hall's Library at, **134**
  Hoys (passenger ships), 135, **136**
Martineau, Harriet, 95, 96, 148, 160
  Illustrations of Political Economy, 160
Marylebone Cricket Club, 111
Marylebone Park, 67
Matlock, 128
Mayfair, 81
Mead, 126
Melbourne, Lord, 166
Mendips, 147
Merchants, **44**

Meredith, George, 153
  Evan Harrington (quoted), 59
Methodists, **139**, 140, 141, 147
Metropolitan Improvements Act (1827), 65
Metropolitan Police Act (1829), 82
Middle classes, Chap. III, **44, 46**
  morality, 138
Middlesex election, **96**
Middleton, 36, 38
Meirs, Mr (silhouette-cutter), 7
Mill, James, 49, 94, 138
Mill, John Stuart, 151, 153
Miner's lamp, Davy's, 158, **159**
Minerva Press novels, 154–6
Mitford, Mary Russell, 155
  Our Village, 122, 137
Mitton, Jack, 53
Monitorial system in schools, 163, 164
Montague, Mr, 117
Moore, George, 32
Moore, Thomas, 142, 146
  Lallah Rookh, 127
Morals, Chap. VI, 138
More, Hannah, 145, 146
  Coelebs in Search of a Wife, 146
  Practical Piety, 146
  Thoughts on the Manners of the Great, 146
More, Martha, 147
Mudeford, 133
Musters, Jack, 53

Nash, Beau, 134
Nash, John, 6, 8, 65, 67ff., 8*5*, 87, 106, **107, 126**
National Scotch Church, London, 144
National Society for Promoting the Education of the Poor, 162
Neate, Bill (prize-fighter), 110
Nelson, Horatio, Viscount, 9
Newgate Jail, **83**
New Lanark, Owen's cotton mill at, **31**, 144
Newman, Cardinal John Henry, 148
Newmarket, 3
'New Rich', the, 54, 139
Newspapers, Stamp duty on, 160
Nicolson, Sir Harold (quoted), 58
Night Life, 78, 79, **80–2**
Norwich, 64
Nottingham, the '11 versus 22' cricket match at (1817), 112
  The Radical March on, 97, 98
  Byron's body at, 143
Novelists, 152–5

Nyrens, the (cricketers), 111

'Officers and gentlemen', **59**, 60
Owen, Robert, 31, **145**
    cotton mill at New Lanark, **31**, 144
    New View of Society (1813), 144
Oxford, Countess of, 104
Oxford University, 164

Paine, Thomas, *The Rights of Man*, 160
Painters, 152
Pall Mall, 78
Palmer, John (mail coach contractor),
    10
Palmer, Samuel (painter), 10
Papworth, J. B., *Rural Residences*, 137
Parliament, 43, 85, **87**, 88, 118
Pedlars, **3**, 4
Peel family (farmer-weavers), 30
Peel, Sir Robert, 82, 86
Penny Encyclopedia, 160
Penny Magazine, 160
Perceval, Spencer, 86, 143
Peterloo, Massacre of, 21, 33, 39, 49,
    93
Petworth, 56
Philosophy, 151
Physician, **59**
Pinkerton, Miss, Academy for Young
    Ladies, 123
Pitt, William, 85, 90, 145
Place, Francis, 15, 92, 93, **94**, 165
Ploughing, **25**
Plumtre, Rev. James, 142
Plymouth, St Andrew's Church, **140**
Podsnap, Mr, 142
Poetry, 151, 152
Police, 82
Political Register, 147
Politics, Chap. V
Poor Law, 144, 149
    Amendment Act (1834), 91
Portugal, 140
Poverty, 22
Powder Tax, 21
Prize-fighting, 4, 60, **109**, **110**
Prosperity, 7
Prostitution, 79, 80, 81, **114**
Provincial Life, Chap. VII
Public schools, **163**, 165
Pückler-Muskau, Prince, 8, 59, 76, 126
Pugin, A. W. N., on Regency building
    (quoted), 144
Puritan Revival, Chap. VIII

Quarterly Review, 156

Radcliffe, Mrs, 153
    Mysteries of Udolpho, 154, 156
    Romance of the Forest, 154
Radicals, 85, 86, 88, 91, **92**, 93, **94**, 95,
    96, **101**
Raikes, Robert, 161
Railways, 1, 132, 135
Randall (pugilist), 110
Ratpit, the Westminster, **18**
Reade, Charles, 152
Reading Public, the new, 153
Reaping, **26**
Recreation, **15**, **57**, **58**, **79–81**, **126–36**
Redesdale, Lord, 53
Reform Bill, 87, 94, 113, 166
'Regency', implications of the term, 1
Regency Theatre, Tottenham Court
    Road, **79**
Regent Street, London, 68, **69**, **72**, **73**, 85
Regent's Canal Company, 13, 68, **76**
    Park, **66**, **67**, **68**, **71**
Religious Observance, 138, 139, **140**,
    141
Religious Tract Society, 146, 148
Repton, Humphrey, 6
Respectability, 140
Reynolds, Sir Joshua, 152
Richmond, Black (prize-fighter), 110
Rickman, Thomas, *Attempt to Discri-
    minate the Styles of English
    Architecture*, 118, 121
Robinson, Henry Crabb, 160
Robinson, P. F., *Designs of Ornamental
    Villas*, 121
    Village Architecture, 121
Rolle Canal, near Torrington, **13**
Romilly (Radical), 92
Royal Institution, **157**
Royal Lancastrian Society, 161
Royal Society, 158
Royal Society for the Prevention of
    Cruelty to Animals, 166
Rugby School, 165
Rural Life, Chap. II
Ruskin, Mr James, 16
Russell, Dr Richard, *Dissertation on the
    Use of Sea Water*, 130

St Andrew's Church, Plymouth, **140**
St John's College, Cambridge, 121
St Katharine's Docks, London, **45**, 76
Sackville, Duke of Dorset (cricketer),
    111
Sam's, Royal Library, Bond Street, **155**

Scarborough, 132
Scarsdale, Lord, 119
Schools, see Education
Science, Popular, 157
Scott, Sir Walter, 95, 107, 151, **152**
Scroggins (prize-fighter), 110
Seaside holidays, 128, **129–34, 136**
Servants, 32, **33**, 127, 140
Sexual behaviour, 104, 105, 138
Seymour, Robert (artist), 2
Shakespeare, William, 79, 142
Sharp, Miss Becky, 139
Shelley, Percy B., 43, 86, 138, 152
Shelton (prize-fighter), 110
Shepherd of Salisbury Plain (tract), **146**
Sherwood, Mrs, 148
Ship-building, 34
Shipping, **45, 76, 77**
Shoemaker, 15, **16**
Shops, **48, 49**
Sidmouth, Henry Addington, Viscount, 86, 88, **89**
Simeon, Dr (preacher), **141**
Slack (prize-fighter), 111
Slave Trade, 145, 149
Slums, development of the, **31**
Smallpox, 17
Smeaton, John (engineer), 62
Smirke, Robert, 69, 75, 118
Smith, Adam, 45, 90
  Wealth of Nations, 162
Smith, Rev. Sydney (quoted), 142, 146
Smollett, Tobias, 154
Soane, Sir John, 6, **75**
Society for the Diffusion of Useful Knowledge, 148, 160
Social injustice in rural areas, 25
Southend-on-Sea, 132, 134, 135
Southey, Robert, 125
Southwark, J. Lancaster's School in, 161
Spa Fields, 96
Spas, **128**, 131, **135**
'Speenhamland System', 26
Spinning cotton, **33, 38**
Sport, 52, 53, **54, 60, 109, 110, 111, 112, 113**
Spring Gardens, London, 81
Spruce beer, 126
Stage coach, **4, 5, 10–13**
Steam power, 14, **15**
Sterne, Laurence, 154
Stevens, 'Lumpy' (cricketer), 111
Stisted Hall, Essex, **8**
Stocking weaver, 15, **16**
Strachey, Lytton, 166
Street traders, 16, **17**

Stretch, Rev. L. M., *Beauties of History*, 124
Strutt, Jedediah, 31
Stubbs, George, Prince of Wales' carriage horses, painted by, **2**
Sunday school, **149**

Taste, decline of, 146
Tea, 127
Telford, Thomas, 10, 62
Textiles, 15, **16, 29, 31, 33**, 35, **36**, 39
Thackeray, William M., 148, 152
  Vanity Fair, 60
Theatre, the, 7, 8, **79, 114**
Thistlewood, Arthur, 99, **100**
Threshing, **25**
Thurtell, John, 81, 110, 139
Tocqueville, Alexis de, 104
Tories, 104, 143
Townshend, Marquess, 105
'Tractarian', 148
Tracts, religious, **146**–8
Transport, 4 ff.
Trulliber, Parson, 141
Tunbridge Wells, 131
Trevithick, Richard, 14
Trimmer, Sarah, 148
Trollope, Anthony, 152
Turner, J. M. W., 152
Twickenham Academy, 124

Underworld, the, 82
Universities, **164**
Upper classe, Chap. III, **50–2, 54–9, 64–75, 80–2**
  fondness for country retreats, 117ff.
  imitation of the lower classes, 108 109
  immorality of, 101, 104
  Manners of, Chap. VI
  sports and pastimes, **53, 54**, 108ff., 111ff.
Ure, Dr Andrew, on child-labour (quoted), 35
  Philosophy of Manufactures (quoted), 48
Utilitarianism, 149
Uttoxeter, 34, 127

Vandyke (racehorse), **3**
Vauxhall Gardens, **81**
Venereal disease, 165
Vice, 102ff.
  Society for the Suppression of, 142

Victoria, Queen, 166, 167
Victorianism, the birth of, 142, 143

Wages, 24, 31, 32
Walpole, Horace (quoted), 131
Waltz, the, 103, **104**
Watch-making, 33
Weare, Mr William, 139
Weaving, 15, **16**, 32, 33, **34**, 36, 37, 38
Wedgwood, Josiah, 158
Wellington, Duke of, 9, 86, 103, 106, 108
Wesley, John, 140, 141
Wesleyan Chapel, Liverpool, **139**
West India Docks, 76, **77**
Westminster Bridge, 62
  Paving and Lighting Act, 78
Westminster Review (quoted), 48, 156
Weymouth, 133
Whaling, whale oil trade, 78
Whigs, 86, 104, 156

Whitefield, George 141
Wilberforce, William, 142, 145, **146**
  Practical Christianity, 145
Wilkes, John, 141
Wilkie, Sir David (painter), 152
  on the middle classes (quoted), 45
Wilkins, William (architect), 69, **164**
Wilson, Harriette, 103, 114–**16**
Winchilsea, Lord, 9
Windham of Felbrigg, 53, 109
Wine, 126
Woodhouse, Mr, 134
Wordsworth, William, 9, 62, 152
Worthing Sands, **130**, **131**
Wyatt, James, 118

Yeoman, the, **24**, 26, **27**
  decline of, 26
York Cottage, 118
Young, Arthur, 145